READINGS ON

THE DIARY OF A YOUNG GIRL

Other titles in the Greenhaven Press Literary Companion Series:

AMERICAN AUTHORS

Maya Angelou
Stephen Crane
Emily Dickinson
William Faulkner
F. Scott Fitzgerald
Nathaniel Hawthorne
Ernest Hemingway
Herman Melville
Arthur Miller
Eugene O'Neill
Edgar Allen Poe
John Steinbeck
Mark Twain

BRITISH AUTHORS

Jane Austen
Joseph Conrad
Charles Dickens

WORLD AUTHORS

Fyodor Dostoyevsky
Homer
Sophocles

AMERICAN LITERATURE

The Great Gatsby
Of Mice and Men
The Scarlet Letter

BRITISH LITERATURE

Animal Farm
The Canterbury Tales
Lord of the Flies
Romeo and Juliet
Shakespeare: The Comedies
Shakespeare: The Sonnets
Shakespeare: The Tragedies
A Tale of Two Cities

THE GREENHAVEN PRESS
Literary Companion
TO WORLD LITERATURE

THE DIARY OF A YOUNG GIRL

David Bender, *Publisher*
Bruno Leone, *Executive Editor*
Brenda Stalcup, *Managing Editor*
Bonnie Szumski, *Series Editor*
Myra H. Immell, *Book Editor*

Greenhaven Press, San Diego, CA

Every effort has been made to trace the owners of copyrighted material. The articles in this volume may have been edited for content, length, and/or reading level. The titles have been changed to enhance the editorial purpose of the Opposing Viewpoints® concept. Those interested in locating the original source will find the complete citation on the first page of each article.

Library of Congress Cataloging-in-Publication Data

Readings on The diary of a young girl / Myra H. Immell, book editor.
         p.   cm. — (Greenhaven Press literary companion to world literature)
    Includes bibliographical references and index.
    ISBN 1-56510-661-X — ISBN 1-56510-660-1 (pbk.)
    1. Frank, Anne, 1929–1945. Achterhuis. 2. Holocaust, Jewish (1939–1945)—Personal narratives—History and criticism. I. Immell, Myra. II. Series.
    DS135.N6F7354   1998
    940.53'18'092—dc21   97-27992
                                                               CIP

Cover photo: Archive Photos

Copyright ©1998 by Greenhaven Press, Inc.
PO Box 289009
San Diego, CA 92198-9009
Printed in the U.S.A.

"I want to live on, even after death."

—*Anne Frank*

CONTENTS

FOREWORD

*"'Tis the good reader that
makes the good book."*

Ralph Waldo Emerson

The story's bare facts are simple: The captain, an old and scarred seafarer, walks with a peg leg made of whale ivory. He relentlessly drives his crew to hunt the world's oceans for the great white whale that crippled him. After a long search, the ship encounters the whale and a fierce battle ensues. Finally the captain drives his harpoon into the whale, but the harpoon line catches the captain about the neck and drags him to his death.

A simple story, a straightforward plot—yet, since the 1851 publication of Herman Melville's *Moby-Dick*, readers and critics have found many meanings in the struggle between Captain Ahab and the whale. To some, the novel is a cautionary tale that depicts how Ahab's obsession with revenge leads to his insanity and death. Others believe that the whale represents the unknowable secrets of the universe and that Ahab is a tragic hero who dares to challenge fate by attempting to discover this knowledge. Perhaps Melville intended Ahab as a criticism of Americans' tendency to become involved in well-intentioned but irrational causes. Or did Melville model Ahab after himself, letting his fictional character express his anger at what he perceived as a cruel and distant god?

Although literary critics disagree over the meaning of *Moby-Dick*, readers do not need to choose one particular interpretation in order to gain an understanding of Melville's novel. Instead, by examining various analyses, they can gain numerous insights into the issues that lie under the surface of the basic plot. Studying the writings of literary critics can also aid readers in making their own assessments of *Moby-Dick* and other literary works and in developing analytical thinking skills.

The Greenhaven Literary Companion Series was created with these goals in mind. Designed for young adults, this unique anthology series provides an engaging and comprehensive introduction to literary analysis and criticism. The essays included in the Literary Companion Series are chosen for their accessibility to a young adult audience and are expertly edited in consideration of both the reading and comprehension levels of this audience. In addition, each essay is introduced by a concise summation that presents the contributing writer's main themes and insights. Every anthology in the Literary Companion Series contains a varied selection of critical essays that cover a wide time span and express diverse views. Wherever possible, primary sources are represented through excerpts from authors' notebooks, letters, and journals and through contemporary criticism.

Each title in the Literary Companion Series pays careful consideration to the historical context of the particular author or literary work. In-depth biographies and detailed chronologies reveal important aspects of authors' lives and emphasize the historical events and social milieu that influenced their writings. To facilitate further research, every anthology includes primary and secondary source bibliographies of articles and/or books selected for their suitability for young adults. These engaging features make the Greenhaven Literary Companion Series ideal for introducing students to literary analysis in the classroom or as a library resource for young adults researching the world's great authors and literature.

Exceptional in its focus on young adults, the Greenhaven Literary Companion Series strives to present literary criticism in a compelling and accessible format. Every title in the series is intended to spark readers' interest in leading American and world authors, to help them broaden their understanding of literature, and to encourage them to formulate their own analyses of the literary works that they read. It is the editors' hope that young adult readers will find these anthologies to be true companions in their study of literature.

INTRODUCTION

*"In spite of everything I believe that people are
really good at heart."*
—Anne Frank

These words—interpreted by millions of people as a testament of faith in humanity—were written by a young girl who died more than fifty years ago. The words come from her diary, first published in English in 1952 under the title *Anne Frank: The Diary of a Young Girl.* Other editions of the diary followed, each longer than the previous edition—thanks to the inclusion of entries that for one reason or another had been omitted before. Thus, each edition is a little more revealing than the one that came before it. The diary, however, remains the *Diary,* no matter the edition.

The articles selected for this volume of the Greenhaven Press Literary Companion Series focus not only on Anne Frank's *Diary* but on Anne Frank herself. With many literary works, it is possible to know the work without knowing the author. But the literary work that is the subject of this volume is a diary, the repository of the innermost thoughts of the diarist. One cannot read *The Diary of a Young Girl* without thinking about—and acknowledging—the girl who wrote it. Anne Frank and her *Diary* are irrevocably intertwined both in fact and in legend.

The articles that make up the main body of this volume span a time period of almost five decades. They are diverse in form—essays, book reviews, academic studies and research papers, introductions to books, magazine and newspaper articles, published narrative. The people who wrote them are equally diverse, both in background and in viewpoint. Some are academics. Some are journalists. Some are writers. Their interpretations of Anne Frank and her *Diary* differ. They do not all agree on what is important about the diary or the diarist. Nor do they all agree on the caliber of the writing or the effectiveness of the writing style. All, however, were sufficiently engaged by the diary to write meaningful commentary about it. Additionally, all the articles are easy to read and very understandable. Their authors let readers know clearly and definitely what their viewpoints are and why they think or feel the way they do.

The Diary of a Young Girl has been translated into more than fifty languages. It has been—and no doubt will continue to be—a source of inspiration for adults and young people all over the world. The editors hope that this volume of the Greenhaven Press Literary Companion Series will add meaning and provide insights into this legendary work and the life of the young girl who wrote it.

ANNE FRANK: A BIOGRAPHY

Anne Frank was a fifteen-year-old German-Jewish victim of the Holocaust who spent more than two years with her parents, sister, and four others hiding in an office building–warehouse in Amsterdam, Holland. Before World War II, about 140,000 Jews lived in Holland, most of them in Amsterdam. About 36,000 survived the Nazi genocide. Anne Frank was not among them. But because of a diary she left behind, she has come to symbolize the millions of Jews who died in World War II—even more, of all people persecuted because of their skin color, background, or beliefs.

Anne Frank was born Anneliese Frank on June 12, 1929, in Frankfurt-am-Main, Germany. Her father, Otto, was a successful banker and businessman. In 1933, Adolf Hitler and his avowedly anti-Semitic Nazi Party came to power and immediately imposed sanctions on Jews ranging from boycotts of Jewish businesses to internment of Jews in Dachau, Hitler's first concentration camp. Frank moved his wife, Edith, and their two young daughters, Margot and Anneliese, from Germany to Amsterdam to escape increasing persecution. The Franks lived comfortably and openly in Holland (known as a country tolerant of Jews) as liberal, assimilated Jews, and Otto Frank established a business selling pectin for household use and, later, various pharmaceuticals and herbs.

In September 1939, World War II erupted with Germany's invasion of Poland. The following year, the Nazis invaded and quickly occupied Holland. Before long, all Dutch people had to carry identity cards. On the cards of all Jews was stamped a large letter *J*. Amsterdam, like the rest of the country, ceased to be a haven. Jews had to wear a large, yellow six-pointed Star of David on their coats and other outer clothes so they could be identified on sight. They were denied access to transportation: They had to relinquish their bicycles and cars and they were denied passage on trains, buses, or in cars driven by others. Many Jews fled the country for England or the United States. Otto Frank chose to stay.

THE SECRET ANNEX

In 1942 the German policy of relocating Jews to urban ghettos switched to mass deportations of Jews to concentration and extermination camps in the occupied territories to the east. In July 1942 Margot Frank received a notice to report to the Dutch Nazi organization. Within days, the Frank family went into hiding in the attic behind Otto's business offices. Miep Gies, an Austrian Christian married to a Dutchman, had worked as Otto Frank's secretary since he first came to Amsterdam in 1933 and agreed to help the family.

Soon others joined the Franks in their hiding place—first, a German couple, Auguste and Hermann Van Pels, and their sixteen-year-old son, Peter, and then a German dentist, Fritz Pfeffer. For two years, while the Jews of Europe were being rounded up and killed, the eight Jews hidden in what Anne called the "Secret Annex" were safe, thanks to Miep Gies and other sympathetic Dutch helpers. Miep, her husband, and three other office workers brought food to the eight residents of the annex, encouraged them, and brought news about the progress of the war.

THE DIARY

Anne Frank celebrated her thirteenth birthday shortly before she and her family went into hiding. The first gift she opened the day of her birthday—Friday, June 12, 1942—was from her parents. It was a small plaid book, a diary. Two days later, she wrote her first entry in it. She continued to write almost every day after that. She explained her feelings about the diary and how important it was to her in this June 20 entry:

> It's an odd idea for someone like me to keep a diary; not only because I have never done so before, but because it seems to me that neither I—nor for that matter anyone else—will be interested in the unbosomings of a thirteen-year-old schoolgirl. Still, what does that matter? I want to write, but more than that, I want to bring out all kinds of things that lie buried deep in my heart. . . .
>
> I don't intend to show this cardboard-covered notebook, bearing the proud name of "diary," to anyone, unless I find a real friend, boy or girl, probably nobody cares. And now I come to the root of the matter, the reason for my starting a diary: it is that I have no such real friend. . . .

> Hence, this diary. In order to enhance in my mind's eye the picture of the friend for whom I have waited so long, I don't want to set down a series of bald facts in a diary like most people do, but I want this diary itself to be my friend, and I shall call my friend Kitty. No one will grasp what I'm talking about if I begin my letters to Kitty just out of the blue.

Anne was to fill the pages of the diary with candid entries filled with wit, insight, and adolescent dreams. She took the diary with her when the family went into hiding, and she wrote in it continually. During her stay in the annex, it remained what Anne had said it would be—her best friend and confidant.

Het Achterhuis

When Anne began writing in her diary, she already was experiencing many of the problems of adolescence. Magnified by her lack of privacy and freedom, her restlessness, vexations, and moodiness were faithfully recorded and, sometimes, dramatized. "I wander from one room to another," she wrote on October 29, 1943, "downstairs and up again, feeling like a songbird whose wings have been clipped and who is hurling himself in utter darkness against the bars of his cage."

In the spring of 1944, Anne heard on the radio that the Dutch government planned to collect war diaries and letters to publish when the war was over. On March 29, she wrote in her diary:

> Mr. Bolkestein, the [Dutch] Cabinet Minister [in exile], speaking on the Dutch broadcast from London, said that after the war a collection would be made of diaries and letters dealing with the war. Of course, everyone pounced on my diary. . . .

> Seriously, though, ten years after the war people would find it very amusing to read how we lived, what we ate and what we talked about as Jews in hiding.

Anne wanted her diary to be one of those published, so she set out to copy it onto single sheets of paper. She cut and revised the entries, polishing and repolishing what she had written, much as a professional writer would. And, envisioning its publication, she gave all the annex occupants pseudonyms in her revised, recopied version, known as version *b*. The Van Pels family became Petronella, Hans, and Alfred Van Daan. Fritz Pfeffer became Alfred Dussel. Anne herself was to be Anne Aulis, or Anne Robin. At the same time, she kept writing in her original diary, which has been called version *a*. On May 11, 1944, she confided to her "Dear Kitty":

Now, about something else: you've known for a long time that my greatest wish is to become a journalist some day and later on a famous writer. Whether these leanings toward greatness (or insanity?) will ever materialize remains to be seen, but I certainly have the subjects in my mind. In any case, I want to publish a book entitled *Het Achterhuis* [*The House Behind*, or *The Secret Annex*] after the war. Whether I shall succeed or not, I cannot say, but my diary will be a great help. I have other ideas as well, besides *Het Achterhuis*. But I will write more fully about them some other time, when they have taken a clearer form in my mind.

A carefree thirteen-year-old when she and her family took refuge in the annex, Anne grew more quiet and pensive daily. Part of the change came from her confinement. Part of it came from her growing maturity. As she matured, so did the diary. It grew into a record of her adolescence, a self-portrait of a talented, insightful girl. The ups and downs of daily life were the focus of her diary—a portrayal of the domestic life led by a group of people with the shadow of death and destruction constantly hanging like a dark and enveloping cloud over them.

DISCOVERY AND DEPORTATION

The occupants of the annex worried all the time that they would be discovered. They heard strange noises and expected to be arrested. The building was burglarized and they expected to be arrested. Finally, on August 4, 1944, about twenty-five months after the Franks first took refuge in the annex, their fears were realized. German SS and Dutch civilian police, believed to be acting on an unidentified informant's tip, entered the Secret Annex and arrested everyone, including the two men who had hidden them. Clearly, someone had betrayed them.

The Franks were transported in a passenger train to Westerbork, the Nazi transit camp for Jews in northern Holland. Some women who knew Anne saw her at the Amsterdam central train station. Said one, "The blue of the sky, the warmth of the sun, all those people being herded into trains ... Anne gazed around her as if she had not seen anyone for a very long time."

On September 3, 1944, the Franks were moved again. This time, there were no passenger trains. They were herded with others into cattle cars and shipped to the Auschwitz death camp in Poland. Otto Frank was separated from his wife and children. More than a decade later, an author named Ernst Schnabel interviewed survivors of the camps who knew Anne Frank. In a 1958 article about Anne and the diary, *Time* magazine reported on Schnabel's findings. According to *Time:*

> At Auschwitz Anne's long hair was clipped and her eyes seemed to grow larger as she grew thinner. Her gaiety disappeared but not her indomitable spirit. The women were divided into groups of five and, though the youngest of her group, Anne became its leader, partly because she was efficient at scrounging necessities. When during cold weather she and the others were reduced to sackcloth smocks, Anne found somewhere a supply of men's long underwear. She even magically produced a cup of coffee for an exhausted prisoner. . . .
>
> Said a survivor: "I can still see her standing by the door, watching a group of naked young gypsy girls being shoved along to the crematory. Anne watched them, weeping, And she also wept when we filed past Hungarian children waiting, twelve hours naked under the rain, for their turn to enter the gas chamber. Anne cried: 'Look at their eyes!' She wept when most of us had no tears left."
>
> On Oct. 30, 1944, there was a selection of the youngest and strongest to be sent to the concentration camp at Bergen. Single file, the undressed women were ordered into a hall where seated behind the glare of a flashlight, a doctor chose this one for Belsen, that one for the gas chamber. "Anne's face remained unchanged, even in the cruel light of the projector. She took Margot's arm and they came forward. I can see them now, stripped naked. Anne turned her serene face toward us; then they were led away. It was impossible to see what happened behind the light, and Mrs. Frank cried, "The children! My God! My God!"

Edith Frank did not go with her daughters. She died in Auschwitz in January 1945 from hunger and exhaustion. Anne and Margot, however, were among the "youngest and strongest" shipped to Bergen-Belsen in northwestern Germany, not far from Hannover. In late February or early March 1945, only six weeks before the British liberated the camp, first Margot and then Anne died of malnutrition and typhus. The bodies of both sisters are believed to have been dumped in the mass graves of Bergen-Belsen.

Anne was not yet sixteen when she died. Her friend Lies Goosens, who survived the war, had been at Bergen-Belsen while Anne was there and saw Anne shortly before she died. She tells how Anne, dressed in a ragged striped uniform "was so emaciated that her eyes were like two pieces of coal deep in the sockets of a skull. Her head was shaved."

A LIFE IN RETROSPECT

In 1993, journalist Marilyn Johnson wrote an article entitled "The Unknown Anne Frank" for *Life* magazine. Her eulogy connected Anne Frank to readers through vivid details:

> She was, in so many ways, an ordinary girl. When she was little, she played in a sandbox. When she grew older, she played Monopoly and Ping-Pong. She rode a bike.
>
> She went to the beach. She had a mom and a dad, a big sister and a cat. The death of her grandmother hit her hard.
>
> She was a skinny little girl with big dark eyes and dimples and thick dark hair. She loved to dress up in pretty clothes and costumes, to curl her hair and try new hairdos. When she was only four, she got all dressed up and went with her dad to his office. She was on her best behavior. She curtsied when she was introduced to the office staff, and while the grown-ups drank coffee, she sipped a glass of milk. Then a young woman who worked in the office volunteered to show her around, and the girl accepted eagerly. She was most interested in a big, black, shiny typewriter. The woman rolled a piece of paper into the machine, then held the girl's tiny fingers against the keys and pressed. Later, the girl and the woman stood at a window, looking down at the people on the street, and the woman, touched by the girl's curiosity and alertness, thought to herself, "Now here's the kind of child I'd like to have someday."
>
> She went to kindergarten at a Montessori school, where her best friend was the little girl next door. In the evening, she and her friend would sit and watch while her dad poured himself a beer. He'd look straight at them, nonchalant, as the beer, rising in the glass, foamed and bubbled and threatened finally to overflow. Amazingly, it always stopped exactly at the top of the glass.
>
> She loved to laugh. She was full of mischief. She was able to pop her shoulder in and out of its socket, and she'd do that occasionally just to alarm people.
>
> She loved going to the movies. She watched reels of Popeye. She watched Shirley Temple and Clark Gable. She loved going to ice-cream parlors. She would order her ice cream between two cookie wafers, then take it out to the sidewalk to eat with her friends. She had lots of friends.
>
> She played with marbles. She played a game something like hopscotch. She said her prayers every night.

Her legs were so thin her socks drooped. When she was sick, which was fairly often, she'd lie in bed near a box filled with pictures of movie stars, princes and princesses.

When she was 11 or 12, she developed a crush on a slim, handsome older boy who had brown eyes and a mischievous laugh. The girl and the boy were inseparable for most of the summer, but then she went off to the countryside for a holiday. When she returned, he was no longer interested in her.

She adored her father, whom everyone described as sweet and patient, but as she grew older she was frequently angry with her mother. She felt her mother misunderstood her, treated her like a baby, was sarcastic, indifferent, unkind. She often cried in bed. Her older sister was smarter and prettier, according to almost everyone: But she was the lively one, the cheeky one. She talked a lot. She talked so much during math, her least favorite class, that the teacher assigned her a paper on the subject of being a chatterbox. Inspired, she wrote that she had inherited a gift for gab from her mother that was incurable.

She fantasized about becoming a writer. She used to sit at her desk in school, scribbling away on a piece of paper with one hand while shielding her words with the other. It drove her school friends crazy that she wouldn't show them what she wrote. For her 13th birthday, her parents gave her a red, white and brown plaid diary to record her thoughts in private. . . .

What happened to the ordinary girl when she was sealed off from the world? She grew like a hothouse flower. She lived on beans and potatoes and rotting vegetables . . . and still managed to grow more than five inches in 25 months. Her eyes deteriorated and she needed eyeglasses that she couldn't get, but she read and wrote almost constantly. As it turned out, she was an incredible writer. At night, she was terrified of bombs and the noise of antiaircraft guns, but in the morning she would slip out of her cot and push aside the black sheet covering the window and sniff at the crack for a little fresh air, and that breath was enough to make her feel awake and alive. She fell in love with the son of the other family in hiding, and got her first kiss in the attic above the secret rooms. . . .

As it turned out, of all the millions of people killed by the Nazis, hers is the name we remember. She would have been 64 this year. She could have been somebody's mother. She could have been just another girl, grown up.

THE DIARY OF A YOUNG GIRL

Thousands of Jews hid from the Nazis during World War II. Like Anne, some of them kept diaries. After the war, more than two hundred of those diaries found their way into Dutch officials' hands alone. But none have had the impact of Anne Frank's diary. First published in 1947, it has sold more than 25 million copies in more than thirty countries. It has been translated into fifty-five languages and is one of the most widely read books in the world next to the Bible. As one journalist succinctly commented, "In terms of public impact, it has no equal."

In 1979 the renowned "Nazi hunter" Simon Wiesenthal, quoted in the *Washington Post*, said that the Anne Frank diary is "more important than the Nuremberg trials." Years later, shortly before apartheid was abolished in his country, South African president Nelson Mandela described how prison inmates would have copies of the *Diary* smuggled in to them because it gave them the will to endure their hardships. In her introduction to the 1993 work *Anne Frank: Beyond the Diary*, Anna Quindlen concurs: "Anne's odyssey of self-interrogation within the confines of the Secret Annex becomes an extraordinary metaphor for life."

When Anne and her sister were taken from Auschwitz, Otto Frank remained behind. He was still there, enfeebled by typhus, when the Germans abandoned the camp in January 1945, shortly before Russian troops liberated it. Weak and grieving, he was repatriated to Amsterdam by way of Odessa and Marseilles. He arrived in Amsterdam on June 3, 1945, the sole survivor of the inhabitants of the annex. When his former secretary and friend Miep Gies invited him to live with her and her husband, he accepted.

Miep and another woman who had helped the Franks when they were in hiding had gone back to the annex after the occupants had been arrested and taken away. There, on the floor of the deserted annex, they discovered the diary, its last entry written three days before the arrest. Miep had taken the diary, which had grown to fill additional notebooks, and put it in a safe place to hold for Anne. She had not read it. When Otto Frank returned to Amsterdam, Miep gave him Anne's diaries. Years later, she was to tell how twice she had risked her own life by going to the Gestapo to try to talk the commanding officer into releasing the Franks.

The papers that Miep Gies gave Frank included both Anne's loose sheets with her revisions and her original diary. Until this point in time, he did not know that Anne had made two versions of her diary. He told a friend:

Of course, I knew that Anna was writing a diary, but she never read parts of it that concerned her personality. In this diary, quite a different Anna appeared to me than the one I used to know. Just as Anna herself wrote in her diary, she didn't want to reveal her inner soul [to us at that time]. So I was very much astonished when I read the deep thoughts she had, her ideals, her courage. . . . In consequence, I believe that most parents don't really know their children.

PUBLICATION OF THE *DIARY*

Using entries from the loose sheets and the diaries, Otto Frank created a manuscript, initially to share with friends and relatives. He did not include all the entries, omitting some that he thought were not very interesting or important. He left out others that he felt were unflattering to his wife or to some of the others in the annex. And he chose to use the Franks' real names but retain pseudonyms—now Petronella, Hermann, and Peter Van Daan, and Alfred Dussel—for the others. Soon, considering the diary Anne's legacy, Otto Frank sought to publish it. He knew that Anne wanted to be a writer, and he wanted her work to contribute to world awareness of Nazi crimes. But finding someone willing to publish the diary proved difficult. More than one publisher told him that the war-weary public did not want to read about the Holocaust. But Otto Frank did not give up easily. One of the people from whom he sought help in finding a publisher was Annie Romein-Vershoor. She could not help him at the time; later, however, she praised the diary for its dual role as a war document and testament of human feeling:

Under the exceptional circumstances of life in the Annex, the growth of the lively, intelligent and impressionable child Anne Frank, from girl to woman, from child to adult, occurred in a remarkably brief time. The relationship of the growing young individual to the outside world, which in normal life is recorded in a great number of more or less fluctuating and varying lines, was here reduced to an extremely simple pattern, forcing her perceptive spirit to expand in depth rather than in width. In a continual process of rapprochement, collision, and wrestling with the seven people around her, in a constant state of inquisitive examination of these seven eternal close-ups, the child's knowledge of human character grew perceptibly. Through introspection forced upon her by circumstances, through a struggle with herself and her limited possibilities, the self-knowledge of the child playing at keeping a diary evolved with unbelievable speed to sharp analysis, even of her own dreams and illusions, of her reactions to her surroundings, of her fate, and of her abandonment of all the beautiful little girl's dreams which were no longer a part of her life in hiding.

There is much more to say about this diary. It is a war document, a document of the cruelty and heartbreaking misery of the persecution of the Jews, of human helpfulness and treason, of human adjustment and non-adjustment, of the small joys and the great and small miseries of life in hiding, written in a direct, non-literary, and therefore often excellent style, by this child who in any case possessed the one important characteristic of a great writer: an open mind, untouched by complacency and prejudice.

But for me the most important thing about this diary is not the documentation, which so often is and will be recorded elsewhere. When people in the tropics take a young plant from the temperate mountain zone and plant it in a very hot area, it will bloom once, richly and superabundantly, only to die soon after. That feeling is what touches me the most in this diary.

In the same way, this small, plucky geranium stood and bloomed, and bloomed, behind the shuttered windows of the Annex.

Annie Romein-Vershoor did give the manuscript to her historian husband, Jan, to read. On April 3, 1946, an article he wrote about the diary was published in the journal *Het Parool.* He had only the highest praise for the diary and for the diarist:

By chance a diary written during the war years has come into my possession. The Netherlands State Institute for War Documentation already holds some two hundred similar diaries, but I should be very much surprised if there were another as lucid, as intelligent, at the same time as natural. This one made me forget the present and its many calls to duty for a whole evening as I read it from beginning to end.

When I had finished it was nighttime, and I was astonished to find that the lights worked, that we still had bread and tea, that I could hear no airplanes droning overhead, no pounding of army boots in the street—I had been so engrossed in my reading, so led away back to that unreal world, now almost a year behind us.

It is written by a Jewish girl who was thirteen years old when she went into hiding with her parents and an older sister and began this diary, and it ends one wretched day more than two years later when the Gestapo discovered the family. One month before Liberation she died in one of the worst German concentration camps, not yet sixteen.

How she died, I do not wish to ask; it was probably in much the same way as has been described in so many camp reminiscences. . . .

The way she died is in any case not important. What matters far more is that her young life was willfully cut short by a system whose witless barbarity we swore never to forget or to forgive while it still raged, but which, now that it belongs to the past, we are already busily, if not forgiving, then forgetting, which ultimately comes to the same thing.

To me, however, this apparently inconsequential diary by a child, this "de profundis" stammered out in a child's voice, embodies all the hideousness of fascism, more so than all the evidence at Nuremberg put together. . . .

If all the signs do not deceive me, this girl would have become a talented writer had she remained alive. Having arrived here at the age of four from Germany, she was able within ten years to write enviably pure and simple Dutch, and showed an insight into the failings of human nature—her own not excepted—so infallible that it would have astonished one in an adult, let alone in a child. At the same time she also highlighted the infinite possibilities of human nature, reflected in humor, tenderness and love, which are perhaps even more astonishing, and from which one might perhaps shrink, especially when they are applied to very intimate matters, were it not that rejection and acceptance remain so profoundly childlike.

That this girl could have been abducted and murdered proves to me that we have lost the fight against human bestiality.

The article created a stir, and Frank had no more trouble finding a publisher. In 1947 Frank's edited manuscript, called version *c*, was published in Holland under the title *Het Achterhuis* (*The Secret Annex*), the title Anne had chosen in her diary. Demand quickly overtook the fifteen hundred copies of the first printing. By 1952 the *Diary* had been translated into German and French, and an English translation had been published in the United States. Neither the Dutch version nor the translations contained all of Anne's entries: The Dutch publisher, Contact, chose not to print certain passages that dealt with Anne's sexuality, and Otto Frank requested that unflattering passages that dealt with Anne's negative feelings about her mother and others in the annex also be omitted.

THE FIRST ENGLISH-LANGUAGE EDITION OF THE *DIARY*

Former first lady of the United States Eleanor Roosevelt wrote the introduction to the English translation—*Anne Frank: The*

Diary of a Young Girl. It quickly became required reading for many American high school students. Wrote Roosevelt:

> This is a remarkable book. Written by a young girl—and the young are not afraid of telling the truth—it is one of the wisest and most moving commentaries on war and its impact on human beings that I have ever read. Anne Frank's account of the changes wrought upon eight people hiding out from the Nazis for two years during the occupation of Holland, living in constant fear and isolation, imprisoned not only by the terrible outward circumstances of war but inwardly by themselves, made me intimately and shockingly aware of war's greatest evil—the degradation of the human spirit.
>
> At the same time, Anne's diary makes poignantly clear the ultimate shining nobility of that spirit. Despite the horror and humiliation of their daily lives, these people never gave up. Anne herself—and, most of all, it is her portrait which emerges so vividly and so appealingly from this book—matured very rapidly in these two years, the crucial years from thirteen to fifteen in which change is so swift and so difficult for every young girl. Sustained by her warmth and her wit, her intelligence and the rich resources of her inner life, Anne wrote and thought much of the time about things which very sensible and talented adolescents without the threat of death will write—her relations with her parents, her developing self-awareness, the problems of growing up.
>
> These are the thought and expression of a young girl living under extraordinary conditions, and for this reason her diary tells us much about ourselves and about our own children. And for this reason, too, I felt how close we all are to Anne's experience, how very much involved we are in her short life and in the entire world.
>
> Anne's diary is an appropriate monument to her fine spirit and to the spirits of those who have worked and are working still for peace. Reading it is a rich and rewarding experience.

Time magazine's reviewer in 1952 agreed: "Anne Frank's entries darkened in tone, her writing skill blossomed, her mind leaped to astonishing maturity. The resulting diary is one of the most moving stories that anyone, anywhere, has managed to tell about World War II."

THE CRITICAL EDITION

Otto Frank died in 1980 at the age of ninety-one. Before his death, he had turned over all of Anne's original papers to the Department of War Documentation of the State of the Netherlands, which took steps to authenticate them. Over the years, various individuals and groups had claimed that the published diary was a hoax, that no young girl Anne's age could write that well. Revisionist groups in particular tried to discredit the diary, claiming that the Holocaust was very much exaggerated or never happened.

The tests were comprehensive. The paper, ink, and glue used in the diary were tested by the Dutch State Forensic Science Laboratory of the Ministry of Justice. So was Anne Frank's handwriting. Experts used forensic techniques to compare the writing in the diary to letters that Anne had written to friends before the war. Dutch scholar David Barnoud was a professor at the Netherlands State Institute for War Documentation and a member of the team that for eight years analyzed the edited and unedited versions of the diaries and instigated the investigation to verify their authenticity. Barnoud attested to the thoroughness of the tests: "We even compared the days she mentioned bomber planes [flew] over her house to records of bombings by the Allies and the Germans. Her observations corroborate with the bombing days."

In 1986, the test results—about 270 pages of them—proving that the diary was not a fake, that the diary actually had been written during the Holocaust by Anne Frank, were published in Holland. Three years later, a summary of the test results, the three diary texts, some of Anne's short stories and sketches, and biographical and historical information about Anne and her family were published in the United States under the title *The Diary of Anne Frank: The Critical Edition*. In an afterword, the question of the authenticity of the diary was definitively addressed: "As far as we are concerned, there is not the slightest reason to doubt either the authenticity of the manuscripts or the intrinsic quality of *The Diary of Anne Frank*."

Hailed as a valuable addition to the literature of the Holocaust, *The Critical Edition* includes all the entries that the original publisher and Otto Frank had omitted from the first edition. It compares the three existing versions of the diary: Anne's original entries, the diary as she edited it when she was in hiding in the Secret Annex, and the version edited by Otto Frank.

THE DEFINITIVE EDITION

Otto Frank had named as his sole heir the Anne Frank-Fonds—the Anne Frank Foundation—which he had established in light of the *Diary*'s worldwide popularity. Part of the inheritance was the copyrights to Anne's writings. The foundation decided to publish a new, expanded edition of the *Diary* for general readers. Writer and translator Mirjam Pressler took on the task of compiling this new edition of the *Diary*.

In 1995, on the fiftieth anniversary of the death of Anne Frank, the new edition was released in the United States. Called *The Diary of a Young Girl: The Definitive Edition*, it was based on Pressler's new English translation of the original Dutch text. According to the foreword, this new edition "in no way affects the integrity of the old one originally edited by Otto Frank, which brought the diary and its message to millions of people. . . . [It] is intended to give the reader more insight into the world of Anne Frank." Thirty percent longer than the 1947 version, this edition restored the entries that had been deliberately omitted earlier. This time Anne Frank's anger, her asides, and her deepest regrets are all included. So are her penetrating commentaries on the failings and lack of insight of adults, the plight of the Jews, anti-Semitism, Germans and Germany, and the overt barbarism of the Nazis.

Most readers and reviewers alike would agree with Kathleen Hughes's review of the *Diary*. After noting that *The Diary of a Young Girl* has been read by millions of people all over the world and is universally acclaimed as a "testament to the resilience of the human spirit, particularly the stoic bravery of a young woman existing in a nightmarish, war-torn world," Hughes comments on the new edition and its restored passages:

> The restored passages serve to emphasize the fact that Anne was, in many ways, a typical teenager. She writes frankly of sexual matters, confides virulent accounts of arguments with her Mother, and pens unflattering (though witty) portraits of other residents of the "Secret Annex." These new additions reveal an intensely real, human Anne Frank. In the more emotional passages, she rages, loves, hates, cries, screams, and hopes. As a result, *The Diary of a Young Girl: The Definitive Edition* is more intensely spellbinding and more heartbreaking and tragic than the original. Those who have already read it in its previous edition as well as readers new to the work will find this version hard to put down.

An Enduring Presence

There is a sad irony in the words Anne, whose body was piled in a mass grave in a long-gone Nazi death camp, penned in her diary on November 11, 1943:

> I went and sat at the table to clear up my writing things, but look as I might, my fountain pen was nowhere to be seen. I looked again. Margot looked, but there was not a trace of the thing. "Perhaps it fell in the stove together with the beans," Margot suggested. "'Oh, no, of course not!" I answered. When my fountain pen didn't turn up that evening, however, we all took it that it had been burned, all the more as celluloid is terribly inflammable.

> And so it was, our unhappy fears were confirmed; when Daddy did the stove the following morning, the clip used for fastening was found among the ashes. Not a trace of the gold nib was found. "Must have melted and stuck to some stone or other," Daddy thought.

> I have one consolation, although a slender one: my fountain pen was cremated, just what I want later!

When Anne wrote in her diary in April 1944, "I want to live on, even after death," she could not have known how powerful a legacy she would leave. Nor could she have known that her dreams of authorship and near immortality would more than come true.

For a time after the war, 263 Prinsengracht, the building that had held the Secret Annex, was used as an office building. But by the late 1950s it was in such bad condition that the 1635 structure was going to be torn down. To avoid its destruction, Otto Frank and others established the Anne Frank House. The preserved building was opened to the public in 1960. Visitors—about 600,000 a year—have been flocking there ever since to see the largely unchanged Secret Annex. The walls of Anne Frank's room still are decorated with the photographs of movie stars that the starstruck teenager tacked up in 1943. The furniture is gone, but Anne Frank's original diaries are on display, and other historically oriented exhibitions—on anti-Semitism, on the history and philosophy of the Nazis, on the Netherlands during World War II, and on modern-day examples of racism and other forms of discrimination—now constitute a museum.

Anne's diary has lived on in other forms as well. There have been media adaptations—a two-act Pulitzer Prize–winning play first produced in New York in 1955, a film released in 1959, and a television movie released in 1980. In 1974 and 1977, selections from the *Diary* were recorded by American actors for release on records and tapes. A 1996 film, *Anne Frank Remembered*, directed by Jon Blair, won the Academy Award for Best Documentary. It brings Anne Frank and the *Diary* to life through the voices of Anne's girlhood friends. Today there are excerpts from the *Diary* on the World Wide Web, as well as various Anne Frank websites, including the home page of the Anne Frank House and Anne Frank Online, sponsored by The Anne Frank Center USA.

Reviewer Alana Suskin, writing for the *Whole Earth Review*, clarifies the vision and gives one answer to the question "Why has Anne Frank become a legend?" "Anne Frank," wrote Suskin,

> has introduced the Holocaust to innumerable people, and her diary has come to be considered a classic. Why is it that we still find ourselves drawn to the writings of this young woman, who has been dead for fifty years?

> Her writing is startling in its clarity and its contemporary sensibilities. But that cannot be all. Anne Frank is compelling because hers is not a tale of endless horror. She is young, and hopeful, she vacillates between believing "in spite of everything, that people are truly good at heart," and that "There's a destructive urge in people, the urge to rage, murder and kill." She is not Everywoman, she is Anne. Her story is her own and no one else's. Yet we relate to Anne Frank because she is like us.

> It becomes easy to run all the tragedies in the world together. It is easy to feel that horror is inevitable, yet for many, Anne Frank brings it back to us, without ever saying explicitly, "Why did you not save me?"

CHAPTER 1

Important Themes in *The Diary of a Young Girl*

Anne as a Role Model for Other Adolescents

Linda Irwin-DeVitis and Beth Benjamin

Linda Irwin-DeVitis and Beth Benjamin are researchers who believe that literature can play an important role in the education and development of adolescent girls. DeVitis and Benjamin assert that through her diary, Anne Frank discloses the struggles of young adolescent girls in general. They used *The Diary of a Young Girl* as a basis for a study they carried out at Binghamton University in Binghamton, New York. In the following discussion of that study, they conclude that young girls today can identify and relate to Anne's struggles, strength, and resolve to preserve her identity and sense of self. They believe that Anne can provide a positive model for teens and that her diary can serve as a forum for reflection on roles and choices potentially available to women.

Anne Frank's diary has been a staple of junior-high and middle-school curricula for several decades. Indeed, one study of most frequently required books in American schools listed it among the top ten selections in public schools for whole class instruction. Traditionally, Anne Frank's story has been taught to highlight issues of the Holocaust and has served as a powerful vehicle for discussion of that historical period. In addition, it has been an excellent basis for exploring issues of racism and prejudice.

We would like to suggest yet another avenue for which *Anne Frank: The Diary of a Young Girl* can be a powerful and provocative basis for discussion—the issue of adolescent girls' development. Anne is expected to be like her older sister, Margot. Adults consider Margot, who is bright but passive and compliant, a model child. Anne's struggles, her

From Linda Irwin-DeVitis and Beth Benjamin, "Can Anne Be Like Margot and Still Be Anne? Adolescent Girls' Development and *Anne Frank: Diary of a Young Girl*," *Alan Review*, vol. 23, no. 1, Fall 1995. Reprinted by permission of the authors and the *Alan Review*.

resolve, and her strength in preserving her identity and sense of self are illuminating and provide a positive model for teens.

FEMALES CREATE "A DIFFERENT TRUTH"

Since the advent of developmental psychology, girls and women, when considered at all, have been a puzzle for theorists and researchers.... Attempts to include girls and women in universal theories have resulted in models that portray girls and women as "less than," incomplete and underdeveloped persons (males), or at best, persons who undergo a development no different from that which occurs for boys and men. Recent research suggests this characterization simply is not the case.

In her groundbreaking examination of girls and young women, Carol Gilligan has posited theories that recognize differences in girls' development [from boys' development].... For Gilligan, women's primary commitment to caring and connection is not a deficiency but a valid alternative to male models that has much value for both the individual and society....

Gilligan and her colleagues in the Harvard Project on Women's Psychology and Girls' Development probed into the developmental crisis that occurs in girls' lives as they move into adolescence. At this point in their lives, girls must reconcile their individuality and growing independence with the strong rhythms of societal expectations and demands. Yet, though girls generally enter this phase with great strength and psychological vigor, the transition from girl to woman is a treacherous one in which many girls begin to doubt their own knowledge and experience, ignore and devalue their own feelings, and move toward relationships based on cultural stereotypes rather than honesty and truth. Gilligan, Lyn Mikel Brown, and their colleagues wanted to explore this crisis of girls' development and find ways in which girls might maintain psychological health and strength as they move into young adulthood....

ANNE'S CONFUSION ABOUT HER ROLE AS A YOUNG WOMAN

For a brief period in early adolescence, usually about age twelve, girls appear to understand the centrality of relationships in their lives; at the same time, they are able to verbalize the frustration they feel when faced with the conflict between being themselves and maintaining their relationships with others. This conflict emerges vividly and poignantly in the pages of *Anne Frank: The Diary of a Young Girl.* As adolescence progresses, Anne Frank, like many young girls, becomes increasingly confused and conflicted about her role as a young woman, and frequently silences herself to fit into a cultural stereotype of womanhood for the sake of relationships. Ironically, however, for Anne, . . . those very relationships are damaged because of the silencing.

As adolescence ensues, girls find themselves less and less able to reconcile their own voices (that is, their wants, needs, interests, and ambitions) with the ideal that society expects and frequently demands. Too often they become convinced that they are lacking and unworthy because they do not measure up to the impossible ideal. In the words of Anne Frank, "I try terribly hard to change myself, but I'm always fighting against a more powerful enemy. . . . A voice sobs within me. . . . 'You are uncharitable, you look supercilious and peevish, people dislike you and all because you won't listen to the advice given you.'"

Anne writes of her longing for someone who could offer "a word of comfort . . . but alas, I keep on looking." The research conducted by Brown and Gilligan . . . suggests that today's female adolescents also seek someone who will acknowledge the reality of their dilemma and recognize their attempts to maintain their real selves in the context of a society working hard to silence them. . . .

ANNE FRANK'S *DIARY* IN THE CLASSROOM

Recognizing the powerful role that literature can play in awareness and education about issues of adolescent girls' development, several researchers have suggested reading lists for adolescent girls. . . .

As teachers become more aware of . . . research findings, they also recognize that much remains to be done if girls are to find an individual niche and voice. A first step for teachers of English would be to include more literature by and about females in the curriculum. A second step would be to change the lenses with which we customarily encourage our students to explore literature. A third would be to open up opportunities for girls to voice their thoughts freely, frequently, and honestly in school settings. . . .

According to a study by Arthur Applebee, the story of

Anne Frank and her family is widely required—in 36% of seventh and eighth grade public school classes and in 56% of classes grades seven through twelve nationwide. It is also required reading in 10% of the nation's Catholic high schools and 14% of independent high schools. Perusal of curriculum guides, however, suggests that the diary is generally treated as a historical tract focusing on issues of the Holocaust rather than as a record of the issues associated with a young girl's entrance into womanhood.

LEARNING ABOUT ADOLESCENCE THROUGH ANNE FRANK'S *DIARY*

We organized a summer literature discussion group that included nine girls, aged 11 to 13, who volunteered to participate. The girls represented four schools from the same community. We took field notes during each conversation and transcribed and analyzed audio tapes of each of the five sessions. The names of the girls have been changed here to ensure confidentiality.

We wanted to know whether young adolescent girls are able to identify, relate to, and speak out about issues of voice when they encounter literature portraying early adolescent females struggling to balance voice and relationship. When given the "prompt" of someone else's experience, would girls see the struggle and discuss it in relation to their own situations? When in a room with only females present and with young female literary figures and characters as the centerpiece of discussion, would they explore the feelings and beliefs that they hold in relation to themselves, their abilities, and their place in their social, familial, and educational worlds?

Believing that Anne's diary could be employed effectively to reach our discussion goals, we selected it as one of the pieces for the discussion group. Although these discussions had a summer informality about them—evening meetings, refreshments, seating around a large table—we wanted to shape them to some extent as reflections of the current thinking about classroom discussion of literature. . . .

We identified three main strategies to support our goals in discussing each book. First, each reader had an opportunity to share her impressions, feelings, and personal connections. The questions we used to begin the conversation were intentionally open-ended and often affective in nature. They included:

- What were your first thoughts as you finished the book?
- Did any parts of this book make you think about an experience of your own?
- Were you reminded of people you know?

Second, the group explored a series of questions on issues of adolescent development as they related to the book.

- How would you describe the female protagonist's attitude about, or outlook on, life?
- Is this girl "nice"? Would your parents or teachers like her?
- Does the female protagonist ever feel that she must sacrifice something important in order to get along with people who are important to her?
- How would this book be different if the female protagonist were male?

Finally, the group analyzed and interpreted quotes (selected by the researchers as relevant to the concerns of female adolescent development) from the book itself. An effort was made to allow the girls to explore the issues of interest to them and to include all of the girls in the discussion. The nine participants in the study shared their perceptions and opinions in regard to Anne and her relationships with others.

ANNE FRANK AS A MODEL

Much of the discussion revolved around girls' deference to societal expectations for young women. . . . Brown and Gilligan argue that this societal mandate pressures girls to subsume their own feelings in consideration of those of others. It constrains them from claiming their own knowledge and teaches them to act and speak cautiously, taking care not to be too forthright, loud, or verbose. . . .

A number of feminist authors and researchers have documented the increasing demands upon young women to live up to images of beauty in the media. As the girls explored the diary, they questioned the societal emphasis on the appearance of girls and women. They felt a connection with Anne, who, feeling outcast, writes in her diary, "Nothing, I repeat, nothing about me is right; my general appearance, my manners are discussed from A to Z."

On the surface, the girls seemed clear that appearance should not be their central concern. Yet their awareness of the importance of looks in our culture and the pervasive influence of the media brought ambivalence and tentativeness to their words. Kara commented, "When you turn on TV, pretty girls with coke . . . [a pretty girl] comes with it. It's like blackmailing."

When asked whether she would rather be known as someone smart or someone good-looking, Sallie responded that she "guessed" she would choose smart, but it "would be nice to be both" although "it doesn't always happen that way." She then indicated in a burst of honesty that her choice might depend on "*how* ugly I'd be!" Mary, in fact the youngest in the group, captured the ambivalence and the dilemma for girls when she stated, "I don't know. I think most girls would say they'd rather be smart," and then quietly added, "but they'd probably rather be pretty."

These girls, like Anne Frank, were torn between what society expects and their own ambitions. Considering her future as an adult female, Anne declares, "I know that I am a woman, a woman with inward strength and plenty of courage. If God lets me live, I shall attain more than Mummy has ever done, I shall not remain insignificant, I shall work in the world, and for mankind." Amy agreed: "You kind of want to be known in your life, not just like your mother." Mary added that she thought Anne Frank and her mother did not get along well due to differing goals. She pointed out that Anne wants to be a writer and then alluded to herself. "I want to be known. I want to be famous." Kara was careful to point out the value of the traditional role of wife and mother even as she envisioned a different goal. "I think for some women, it's their lifetime goal to have children. I think women should have the choice, but it's not what I want." These young women were already grappling with their own desires and attempting to separate the rhetoric of women's choice from the reality of their own experience and that of their mothers. Anne's diary provided a forum for their reflection on the roles and choices potentially available to women.

IF ANNE HAD BEEN A BOY

Their own experiences had clearly led them to understand that there are different societal expectations for young women and young men. While these girls, particularly Kara, were articulate about the choices available to women and the progress in the area of women's rights, they were also keenly aware that males are still rewarded for speaking up and voicing their opinions while girls are not. When asked how the diary would have been different if the author had been a male, the girls did not hesitate:

> Jackie: It would be a whole different story.
>
> Mary: I don't think they would criticize [the diary's author] as much if it had been written by a boy.
>
> Kara: Seeing how the Van Daans treated Peter, he would be allowed his opinions . . . would be listened to. I think the problems they have with Anne is that she talks too much about what she thinks.
>
> Mary: I think the reason why her mom is not happy with Anne is because Anne is not the way her mother wants her to be. And if she were a boy, it wouldn't matter. She really might not expect as much. . . . Anne was expected to be quiet, but maybe a boy wouldn't be like a prisoner.

The girls perceived the gender-bound expectations of their parents and society, expectations that Anne Frank, too, outlines, "One must apply one's reason to everything here, learning to obey, to hold your tongue, to help, to be good, to give in, and I don't know what else." Anne rages against the role she is assigned, resenting the mandates of obedience, submission, and self-sacrifice.

Anne Frank's words resonated with these girls who also felt the pressure to be passive, to obey, and to please others. Mary wistfully acknowledged the possibility of finding unqualified acceptance, but her voice was tentative and full of doubt. "They expect you to be good . . . they're proud of you. If you weren't good for them . . . I don't know . . . maybe they would still find the good in you."

ANNE IS NOT MARGOT

At times the girls puzzled over their desire to be strong, courageous, and outspoken contrasted with the adult expectation that they be submissive and silent. In sharing an account of an incident from her fifth grade year, Sallie expressed both pride and embarrassment, possibly even a hint of shame, in relation to the stance she took and the outcome that ensued. Sallie knew, as early as fifth grade, that "nice" girls should not prove adults wrong. Telling the tale three years later, she frequently employed a questioning tone that indicated uncertainty about her actions.

> Sallie: At one point I did, um, stand up for myself. They were sending me down to a special class to work on my math. And I didn't need it. I needed reading help. And, um, I just stood

there and wouldn't go. I insisted I am not going into the room. And then I was sent from there . . . and sat in the office. And so we had a parent-teacher conference of seven teachers, my parents, and the principal! . . . Luckily, I got taken out of that class. They ended up giving a test for that grade . . . and I ended up being on an eighth-grade math level but a third-grade reading level, so they decided they would help me in reading.

Researcher: Were you glad you stuck up for yourself?

Sallie: In a way, and then—in a way, I didn't. Well, um, I guess I just, um, I guess it was just that I felt bad that I was kinda right, in a way, I sort of wished I was wrong, but in another way I wasn't. I was trying . . . , hoping to prove the teachers wrong. And when I did [giggle] I just felt bad. . . . You're not supposed to prove teachers wrong.

Sallie's confusion over this incident exemplifies a key dilemma identified by Brown and Gilligan . . . : how can an adolescent girl speak out with honesty and remain true to herself, yet not sacrifice relationships? For all of the girls in our discussion group, this conflict between being oneself and being what others expect loomed large. Amy captured the dilemma succinctly when she pondered, "Can Anne still be Anne and be like Margot?" Sallie, who continues to wonder if she did the right thing in fifth grade, seemed to feel that a split personality could be a solution. "Anne could *act* like her sister, but she herself [would know] she really isn't her sister. I can act like my sister and still be me." Yet even in suggesting this duality, she vacillated as she went on to say, "[But] after a while I would speak up. I wouldn't keep as quiet as [Anne's] sister. That's a bit quiet." As the girls teetered back and forth between what they knew to be right and what society urged them to forget, they appeared to be capitulating to societal stereotypes. . . .

Anne's growing need to be accepted by family and friends, to conform to expectations, and the resulting pressure to stifle her own ideas rang true to the girls in our group and emerged as a real issue for them. They discussed the journal entry where Anne Frank wrote,

> I might tell you I don't want to be in the least like Margot. She is much too soft and passive for my liking and allows everyone to talk her around, and gives in about everything. I want to be a stronger character! But I keep such thoughts to myself: they would only laugh at me, if I came along with this as an explanation of my attitude.

The girls identified with Anne's silent resistance to the role of the model child and her resentment of the praise heaped upon her older sister for playing the part so well.

> Mary: Anne has a lot of pressure. She's always trying harder.
> Everyone wants her to be like her older sister. She's different.
> Margot is a model child. She's under a lot of pressure to be
> like her, not to be herself.

Researcher: Model child?

> Kara: One that doesn't argue, one who is smart, but doesn't
> voice her opinion. . . .

ANNE'S STRONG AND ASSERTIVE STANCE

Early in Anne Frank's diary, she demonstrates a remarkably
strong and assertive stance. Her sense of self is palpable
when she writes,

> I'm expected (by order) simply to swallow all the harsh
> words and shouts in silence and I am not used to this. In fact,
> I can't! I'm not going to take all these insults lying down. . . .
> Am I really so bad-mannered, conceited, headstrong, push-
> ing, stupid, lazy, etc., etc., as they all say? Oh, of course not. I
> have my faults, just like everyone else, I know that, but they
> thoroughly exaggerate everything.

and

> It is hard to speak the truth, and yet it is truth: she [Anne's
> mother] herself has pushed me away, her tactless remarks
> and crude jokes. . . . They expect me to apologize; but this is
> something I can't apologize for because I spoke the truth and
> Mummy will have to know it sooner or later anyway.

Yet, as months in the Secret Annexe pass, Anne begins to
worry that she is losing the fight to be herself, to speak out
and speak truth.

> This "self-consciousness" haunts me, and every time I open
> my mouth I know as soon as I've spoken whether "that ought
> to have been different" or "that was right as it was."

Through her diary Anne Frank discloses the struggle
faced by the girls in our group and identified by Shea, that of
"defining themselves within a web of relationships." These
girls are faced with choices between maintaining themselves
and speaking the truth as they see it and the growing real-
ization that such honesty jeopardizes the relationships that
they also prize. Like Anne, they are in danger of having their
real selves shrivel up and disappear. Like Anne, although
without exception they expressed strong preferences for
being defined by their intelligence, wit, and character, they
have started to frame their answers in deference to their desire to maintain relationships. Like Anne when she says, "I

never utter my real feelings about anything ... and [I] keep on trying to find a way of becoming what I would so like to be, and what I could be if ... there weren't any other people living in the world," they fight to preserve their intelligence and strength, though they are often in Debold's words, "betrayed by a culture that doesn't really want either."

The girls in our discussion chafed at the unfairness of Anne Frank's treatment. ... "They should leave her alone. I think she was fine the way she was." Jenny was convinced that if the people in Anne's life would try to "understand her, let her talk, then they'd like her." We could all benefit from Jenny's wisdom. If we care about girls and truly want to understand them, we must provide opportunities for them to talk about the issues of growing up female that are so real and relevant.

REFERENCES

Arthur Applebee, *A Study of Book-Length Works Taught in High School English Courses.* (Report Series No. 1.2). Center for the Learning and Teaching of Literature, University at Albany, State University of New York, 1989.

Lyn Mikel Brown, and Carol Gilligan, *Meeting at the Crossroads: Women's Psychology and Girls' Development.* Cambridge, MA: Harvard University Press, 1992.

Elizabeth Debold, Marie Wilson, and Idelisse Malave, *Mother Daughter Revolution: From Betrayal to Power.* Reading, MA: Addison Wesley, 1993.

Carol Gilligan, *In a Different Voice: Psychological Theory and Women's Development.* Cambridge, MA: Harvard University Press, 1982.

Renee H. Shea, "Gilligan's 'Crisis of Connections': Contemporary Caribbean Women Writers," *English Journal,* 81.1, 1992, pp. 36–41.

The *Diary* Speaks for Millions of Jews

Meyer Levin

Meyer Levin is a Jewish-American writer and filmmaker who became obsessed with Anne Frank's *Diary*. With expectations of receiving rights to an American dramatic adaptation of the *Diary*, he prepared the script of a play based on it. When the script was judged structurally and dramatically weak and someone else was given the stage rights, Levin began a long vendetta against everyone involved, including Anne Frank's father, Otto Frank. Levin wrote the following article shortly after the first English translation of the *Diary* was published. In the article, he contends that the diary holds a double significance. On one level, it is a poignantly classic portrait of a young girl growing into womanhood under "astonishing circumstances." On another, the voice of its author represents the voice of the millions of Jews who did not survive the Holocaust.

Anne Frank's *Diary* is too tenderly intimate a book to be frozen with the label "classic," and yet no lesser designation serves. For little Anne Frank, spirited, moody, self-doubting, succeeded in communicating in virtually perfect, or classic, form the drama of puberty. But her book is not a classic to be left on the library shelf. It is a warm and stirring confession, to be read over and over for insight and enjoyment.

The diary is a classic on another level, too. It happened that during the two years that mark the most extraordinary changes in a girl's life, Anne Frank lived in astonishing circumstances: she was hidden with seven other people in a secret nest of rooms behind her father's place of business, in Amsterdam. Thus, the diary tells the life of a group of Jews waiting in fear of being taken by the Nazis. . . .

From Meyer Levin, "The Child Behind the Secret Door," *New York Times Book Review*, June 15, 1952, pp. 1, 22. Copyright ©1952 by the New York Times Company. Originally appeared in *The New York Times Book Review*. Reprinted by permission of the author's estate and its agents, Scott Meredith Literary Agency, L. P., 845 Third Avenue, New York, New York, 10022.

This is no lugubrious ghetto tale, no compilation of horrors. Reality can prove surprisingly different from invented reality, and Anne Frank's diary simply bubbles with amusement, love, discovery. It has its share of disgust, its moments of hatred, but it is so wondrously alive, so near, that one feels overwhelmingly the universalities of human nature. These people might be living next door; their within-the-family emotions, their tensions and satisfactions are those of human character and growth, anywhere.

Because the diary was not written in retrospect, it contains the trembling life of every moment—Anne Frank's voice becomes the voice of six million vanished Jewish souls. It is difficult to say in which respect her book is more "important," but one forgets the double significance of this document in experiencing it as an intimate whole, for one feels the presence of this child-becoming-woman as warmly as though she was snuggled on a near-by sofa.

CONFIDENCES OF A THIRTEEN-YEAR-OLD

We meet Anne on her thirteenth birthday, "Quicksilver Anne" to her adored father, but "Miss Chatterbox" and "Miss Quack-Quack," she tells us to her teacher—for the family is still at liberty. Indeed, her teacher makes her write a self-curing essay on chattering; she turns in a poem that convulses teacher and class, and is allowed to remain her talkative self without further reprimand.

Yet, with the moodiness of adolescence, she feels lonesome. "Let me put it more clearly, since no one will believe that a girl of 13 feels herself quite alone in the world, nor is it so. I have darling parents and a sister of 16. I know about 30 people whom one might call friends—I have strings of boyfriends, anxious to catch a glimpse of me, who . . . peep at me through mirrors in class. I have relations, aunts, uncles, who are darlings too, a good home, no—I don't seem to lack anything. But it's the same with all my friends, just fun and joking, nothing more. I can never bring myself to talk of anything outside the common ground. We don't seem to be able to get any closer, that is the root of the whole trouble. Hence, this diary. I want this diary itself to be my friend, and shall call my friend Kitty."

What child of 13 hasn't had these feelings, and resolved to confide in a diary? Anne carried it through, never shrinking from revealing the ugly things about herself.

Her father had already brought the family out of Germany in 1933. In June, 1942, a few weeks after the diary begins, the SS sends a call-up for Anne's sister, Margot, and the family goes into hiding. "I began to pack some of our most vital belongings into a school satchel . . . this diary, then hair curlers, handkerchiefs, schoolbooks, a comb, old letters." The Van Daans, with their 16-year-old son Peter, join the Franks. Later, because "Daddy says we must have another person if we can," an elderly dentist named Dussel is squeezed into the Secret Annex. He gets Anne's bed; she sleeps on a settee lengthened by chairs.

A born writer, Anne zestfully portrays the Annex inhabitants, with all their flaws and virtues. The common life effect . . . flowers with utter spontaneity. But Anne Frank's diary probes . . . into the core of human relations in bringing us an understanding of life under threat.

And this quality brings it home to any family in the world today. Just as the Franks lived in momentary fear of the Gestapo's knock on their hidden door, so every family today lives in fear of the knock of war. Anne's diary is a great affirmative answer to the life question of today, for she shows how ordinary people, within this ordeal, consistently hold to the greater human values.

The Franks' Dutch friends in the office on the other side of the secret door sustained them to the end. "Never have we heard *one* word of the burden which we certainly must be to them . . . they put on the brightest possible faces, bring flowers and presents for birthdays, risking their own lives to help others." These Dutch friends, Miep, Elli, Kraler, Koophuis, even managed to smuggle in Chanukah gifts, and shyly offered their Christmas remembrances to the hidden Jews.

Two years passed in disciplined activities. The hidden ones kept busy with smuggled correspondence courses in speed shorthand, in Latin, in nursing: Dussel even attempted dental operations, hilariously described by Anne. She herself studied mythology, ballet, "family trees," while keeping up her school work. She records the family disputes—Mrs. Van Daan violently resisting the sale of her fur coat, only to see it smoked up in black market tobacco! And the comic moments, as when her father lies on the floor trying to overhear an important business conference downstairs; Anne flattens herself beside him, lending a sharp ear. But business is so dull, she falls asleep.

Most wondrous of all is her love affair. Like a flower under a stone fulfilling itself, she came to her first love in her appointed time. "I give myself completely. But one thing. He may touch my face but no more." All is told from her potato-fetching devices for going up to Peter's attic lair, to the

---

WHEN IT COMES TO SEX

On Saturday, March 18, 1944, Anne Frank confided to her "Dearest Kitty" her feelings about sex. Her opinions on the subject remain universal, shared by many adolescent girls then and now.

SATURDAY, MARCH 18, 1944

Dearest Kitty,

I've told you more about myself and my feelings than I've ever told a living soul, so why shouldn't that include sex?

Parents, and people in general, are very peculiar when it comes to sex. Instead of telling their sons and daughters everything at the age of twelve, they send the children out of the room the moment the subject arises and leave them to find out everything on their own. Later on, when parents notice that their children have, somehow, come by their information, they assume they know more (or less) than they actually do. So why don't they try to make amends by asking them what's what?

A major stumbling block for the adults—though in my opinion it's no more than a pebble—is that they're afraid their children will no longer look upon marriage as sacred and pure once they realize that, in most cases, this purity is a lot of nonsense. As far as I'm concerned, it's not wrong for a man to bring a little experience to a marriage. After all, it has nothing to do with the marriage itself, does it?

Soon after I turned eleven, they told me about menstruation. But even then, I had no idea where the blood came from or what it was for. When I was twelve and a half, I learned some more from Jacque, who wasn't as ignorant as I was. My own intuition told me what a man and a woman do when they're together; it seemed like a crazy idea at first, but when Jacque confirmed it, I was proud of myself for having figured it out!

It was also Jacque who told me that children didn't come out of their mother's tummies. As she put it, "Where the ingredients go in is where the finished product comes out!".... When I came here, Father told me about prostitutes, etc., but all in all there are still unanswered questions.

If mothers don't tell their children everything, they hear it in bits and pieces, and that can't be right....

Yours, Anne M. Frank

first misplaced kiss, on her ear. And the parents worrying about the youngsters trysting up there in the dusk, sitting by the window over the canal. And her fears that her older sister is lonely and jealous, leading to an amazing exchange of letters between the two girls, in those hidden rooms. Finally, there is even the tender disillusionment with Peter, as Anne reaches toward maturity, and a character understanding replaces the first tug of love. In all this there are perceptions in depth, strivings toward mother, father, sister, containing love-anguish of the purest universality.

As is arch-typical for a girl in this period, her relations with her mother are difficult. Unflinchingly, Anne records each incident.

> Dear Kitty—Oh dear, I've got another terrible black mark against my name. I was lying in bed yesterday evening waiting for Daddy to come and say my prayers with me, and wish me good night, when Mummy came into my room, sat on my bed, and asked very nicely, "Anne, Daddy can't come yet, shall I say your prayers with you tonight?" "No, Mummy," I answered.
>
> Mummy got up, paused by my bed for a moment, and walked slowly toward the door. Suddenly she turned around, and with a distorted look on her face said, "I don't want to be cross, love cannot be forced." There were tears in her eyes as she left the room.
>
> I lay still in bed, feeling at once that I had been horrible to push her away so rudely. . . . It is hard to speak the truth, yet it is the truth: she herself has pushed me away, her tactless remarks and her crude jokes, which I don't find at all funny, have now made me insensitive to any love from her side.

THE MATURATION OF ANNE FRANK

But her understanding grew, until she could write, "The period when I caused Mummy to shed tears is over. I have grown wiser and Mummy's nerves are not so much on edge."

It is this unfolding psychological drama of a girl's growth, mingled with the physical danger of the group, that frees Anne's book from the horizontal effect of most diaries. Hers rises continuously, with the tension of a well-constructed novel. On the plane of physical suspense, a series of burglaries in the office-warehouse dreadfully endangers the hidden group. And there is the race of the Nazis' intensified hunt for victims, as against the progress of the Allied campaign, followed over a clandestine radio.

Psychologically, the diary contains the completely rounded story of the development of a social nature; one lives in suspense, watching it unfold: will she understand her mother? will she surmount her perplexities? will she comprehend her body-changes, so frankly described?

The girl's last entries rather miraculously contain a climactic summation, a maturing self-analysis: "If I'm quite serious, everyone thinks it's a comedy, and then I have to get out of it by turning it into a joke," she remarks with typical adolescent self-consciousness. "Finally I twist my heart around again, so that the bad is on the outside and the good is on the inside. . . . I am guided by the pure Anne within, but outside I am nothing but a frolicsome little goat who's broken loose."

This frolicsome little goat could write, "It's twice as hard for us young ones to hold our ground, and maintain our opinions, in a time when all ideals are being shattered and destroyed, when people are showing their worse side, and do not know whether to believe in truth and right and God."

> It's really a wonder that I haven't dropped all my ideals, because they seem so absurd and impossible to carry out. Yet I keep them, because in spite of everything I still believe that people are really good at heart. I simply can't build up my hopes on a foundation consisting of confusion, misery, and death. I see the world gradually being turned into a wilderness. I hear the ever-approaching thunder, which will destroy us too, I can feel the sufferings of millions and yet, if I look up into the heavens, I think that it will all come right, that this cruelty too will end, and that peace and tranquility will return again.

"I want to go on living even after my death," Anne wrote. "I am grateful to God for giving me this gift, this possibility of developing myself and of writing, of expressing all that is in me." Hers was perhaps one of the bodies seen in the mass grave at Bergen-Belsen, for in August, 1944, the knock came on that hidden door in Amsterdam. After the people had been taken away, Dutch friends found Anne's diary in the debris, and saved it.

There is anguish in the thought of how much creative power, how much sheer beauty of living, was cut off through genocide. But through her diary Anne goes on living. From Holland to France, to Italy, Spain. The Germans too have published her book. And now she comes to America. Surely she will be widely loved, for this wise and wonderful young girl brings back a poignant delight in the infinite human spirit.

The Development of Anne Frank

John Berryman

John Berryman was a professor at the University of
Minnesota and a Pulitzer Prize–winning poet. The
following essay from his collection *Freedom of the
Poet* was devoted to the process of the development
of Anne Frank, whose *Diary* he thought was universally valued for the wrong reasons. Berryman sets
out to show that the physical and psychological context of Anne Frank's development and the personal
qualities she brought to her situation were necessary
conditions of that development. For Berryman, the
Diary can be described as "the conversion of a child
into a person."

When the first installment of the translated text of *The Diary
of Anne Frank* appeared in the spring of 1952, in *Commentary*, I read it with amazement. The next day, when I went
into town to see my analyst, I stopped in the magazine's offices—I often did, to argue with Clem Greenberg, who was
a sort of senior adviser to what was at that time the best general magazine in the country in spite of, maybe because of,
its special Jewish concerns—to see if proofs of the *Diary*'s
continuation were available, and they were. Like millions of
people later, I was bowled over with pity and horror and admiration for the astounding doomed little girl. But what I
thought was: a sane person. A sane person, in the twentieth
century. It was as long ago as 1889 when Tolstoy wound up
his terrible story "The Devil" with this sentence:

> And, indeed, if Evgeni Irtenev was mentally deranged, then
> all people are mentally deranged, but undoubtedly those are
> most surely mentally deranged who see in others symptoms
> of insanity which they fail to see in themselves.

Some years later (1955), setting up a course called "Human-
ities in the Modern World" at the University of Minnesota, I

assigned the *Diary* and reread it with feelings even more powerful than before but now highly structured. I decided that it was the most remarkable account of *normal* human adolescent maturation I had ever read, and that it was universally valued for reasons comparatively insignificant. I waited for someone to agree with me. An article by Bettelheim was announced in *Politics*, appeared, and was irrelevant. The astute Alfred Kazin and his wife, the novelist Ann Birstein, edited Anne Frank's short fiction—ah! I thought—and missed the boat.

Here we have a book only fifteen years old, the sole considerable surviving production of a young girl who died after writing it. While decisively rejecting the proposal—which acts as a blight in some areas of modern criticism—that a critic should address himself only to masterworks, still I would agree that some preliminary justification seems desirable.

It is true that the book is world-famous. I am not much impressed by this fact, which I take to be due in large part to circumstances that have nothing to do with art. The author has been made into a spokesman against one of the grand crimes of our age, and for her race, and for all its victims, and for the victims (especially children) of all the tyrannies of this horrifying century,—and we could extend this list of circumstances irrelevant to the *critical* question. Some proportion of the book's fame, moreover, is even more irrelevant, as arising from the widespread success of a play adapted from it, and a film. That the book *is* by a young girl—an attractive one, as photographs show—must count heavily in its sentimental popularity. And, finally, the work has decided literary merit; it is vivid, witty, candid, astute, dramatic, pathetic, terrible,—one falls in love with the girl, one finds her formidable, and she breaks one's heart. All right. It is a work infinitely superior to a similar production that has been compared to it, *The Diary of "Helena Morley,"* beautifully translated by Elizabeth Bishop in 1957. Here is a favourable specimen of the Brazilian narrative:

> When I get married I wonder if I'll love my husband as much as mama loves my father? God willing. Mama lives only for him and thinks of nothing else. When he's at home the two spend the whole day in endless conversation. When papa's in Boa Vista during the week, mama gets up singing wistful love songs and we can see she misses him, and she passes the time going over his clothes, collecting the eggs, and fattening

the chickens for dinner on Saturday and Sunday. We eat best on those days.

FROM CHILD INTO PERSON

Clearly the temperature here is nothing very unusual, and no serious reader of Anne Frank, with her extraordinary range and tension, will entertain any comparison between the two writers. But I am obliged to wonder whether Anne Frank has *had* any serious readers, for I find no indication in anything written about her that anyone has taken her with real seriousness. A moment ago we passed, after all, the critical question. *One finds her formidable:* why, and how, ought to engage us. And first it is necessary to discover what she is writing about. Perhaps, to be sure, she is not truly writing about anything—you know, "thoughts of a young girl," "Jews in hiding from the Nazis," "a poignant love affair"; but such is not my opinion.

Suppose one became interested in the phenomenon called religious conversion. There are books one can read. There is one by Sante de Sanctis entitled *Religious Conversion*, there are narratives admirably collected in William James's lectures, *The Varieties of Religious Experience*, there is an acute account of the most momentous Christian conversion, Paul's, by Maurice Goguel in the second volume (*The Birth of Christianity*) of his great history of Christian origins. If one wants, however, to experience the phenomenon, so far as one can do so at second hand,—a phenomenon as gradual and intensely reluctant as it is also drastic,—there is so far as I know one book and one only to be read, written by an African fifteen hundred years ago. Now in Augustine's *Confessions* we are reckoning with just one of a vast number of works by an architect of Western history, and it may appear grotesque to compare to even that one, tumultuous and gigantic, the isolated recent production of a girl who can give us nothing else. A comparison of the *authors* would be grotesque. But I am thinking of the originality and ambition and indispensability of the two books *in the heart of their substances*,—leaving out of account therefore Book X of the *Confessions*, which happens to award man his deepest account of his own memory. I would call the subject of Anne Frank's *Diary* even more mysterious and fundamental than St Augustine's [*Confessions*], and describe it as: the conversion of a child into a person.

At once it may be exclaimed that we have thousands of books on this subject. I agree: autobiographies, diaries, biographies, novels. They seem to me those that in various literatures I have come on—to bear the same sort of relation to the *Diary* that the works *on* religious conversion bear to the first seven books of the *Confessions*. Anne Frank has made the process itself available.

Why—I asked myself with astonishment when I first encountered the *Diary,* or the extracts that *Commentary* published—has this process not been described before? Universal as it is, and universally interesting? And answers came. It is *not* universal, for most people do not grow up, in any degree that will correspond to Anne Frank's growing up; and it is *not* universally interesting, for nobody cares to recall his own, or can. It took, I believe, a special pressure forcing the child-adult conversion, and exceptional self-awareness and exceptional candour and exceptional powers of expression, to bring that strange or normal change into view. This, if I am right, is what she has done, and what we are to study.

TWO SETS OF CONDITIONS OF DEVELOPMENT

The process of her development, then, is our subject. But it is not possible to examine this without some prior sense of two unusual sets of conditions in which it took place: its physical and psychological context, first, and second, the qualities that she took into it. Both, I hope to show, were *necessary* conditions.

For the context: it was both strange, sinister, even an "extreme situation" in Bettelheim's sense, and pseudo ordinary; and it is hard to say which aspect of the environment was more crippling and crushing. We take a quicksilver-active girl thirteen years old, pretty, popular, voluble, brilliant, and hide her, as it were, in prison; in a concealed annex upstairs at the rear of the business premises her father had commanded; in darkness, behind blackout curtains; in slowness—any movement might be heard—such that after a time when she peeks out to see cyclists going by they seem to be flying; in closeness—not only were she and her parents and sister hopelessly on top of each other, but so were another family with them, and another stranger—savagely bickering, in whispers, of course; in fear—of Nazis, of air raids, of betrayal by any of the Dutch who knew (this, it seems, is what finally happened, but the marvellous goodness of the responsible Dutch is one of the themes of the *Diary*), of thieves (who came),—the building, even, was once sold out from under them, and the new owner simply missed the entrance to their hiding place. All this calls for heroism, and it's clear that the personalities of the others except Mr. Frank withered and deteriorated under conditions barely tolerable. It took Anne Frank herself more than a year to make the sort of "adjustment" (detestable word) that would let her free for the development that is to be our subject.

But I said, "as it were, in prison." To prison one can become accustomed; it is *different*, and one has no responsibilities. Here there was a simulacrum of ordinary life: she studied, her family were about her, she was near—very near—the real world. The distortion and anxiety are best recorded in the dreadful letter of 1 April 1943. Her father was still (sort of) running the company and had briefed his Dutch assistant for an important conference; the assistant fell ill and there wasn't time to explain "fully" to his replacement; the responsible executive, in hiding, "was trembling with anxiety as to how the talks would go." Someone suggested that if he lay with his face on the floor he might hear. So he did, at 10:30 a.m., with the other daughter, Margot, until 2:30, when half paralyzed he gave up. The daughters took over, understanding scarcely a word. I have seldom, even in modern literature, read a more painful scene. It takes Anne Frank, a concise writer, thirteen sentences to describe.

Let's distinguish, without resorting to the psychologists, temperament from character. The former would be the disposition with which one arrives in the world, the latter what has happened to that disposition in terms of environment, challenge, failure and success, by the time of maturity,—a period individually fixed between, somewhere between, fifteen and seventy-five, say. Dictionaries will not help us; try Webster's Dictionary of Synonyms if you doubt it. Americans like dictionaries, and they are also hopeless environmentalists (although they do not let it trouble their science, as Communists do). I ought therefore perhaps to make it plain that children do differ. The small son of one of my friends would cheerfully have flung himself off the observation tower of the Empire State Building. The small son of another friend was taking a walk, hand in hand, with his father, when they came to an uneven piece of sidewalk and his father heard him say to himself, "now, Peter, take it easy,

Peter, that's all right, Peter," and they went down the other end of the slightly tilted block. My own son, a friend of both, is in between, Dionysiac with the first, Apollonian with Peter. I think we ought to form some opinion of the *temperament* of Anne Frank before entering on her ordeal and thereafter trying to construct a picture of her character.

ANNE'S TEMPERAMENT

The materials are abundant, the *Diary* lies open. She was vivacious but intensely serious, devoted but playful. It may later on be a question for us as to whether this conjunction "but" is the right conjunction, in her thought. She was imaginative but practical, passionate but ironic and cold-eyed. Most of the qualities that I am naming need no illustration for a reader of the *Diary:* perhaps "cold-eyed" may have an exemplar: "Pim, who was sitting on a chair in a beam of sunlight that shone through the window, kept being pushed from one side to the other. In addition, I think his rheumatism was bothering him, because he sat rather hunched up with a miserable look on his face . . . He looked exactly like some shriveled-up old man from an old people's home." So much for an image of the man—her adored father—whom she loves best in the world. She was self-absorbed but un-self-pitying, charitable but sarcastic, industrious but dreamy, brave but sensitive. Garrulous but secretive; skeptical but eloquent. This last "but" may engage us, too. My little word "industrious," like a refugee from a recommendation for a graduate student, finds its best instance in the letter, daunting to an American student, of 27 April 1944, where in various languages she is studying in one day matters that—if they ever came up for an American student—would take him months.

The reason this matters is that the process we are to follow displays itself in a more complicated fashion than one might have expected: in the will, in emotion, in the intellect, in libido. It is surprising what it takes to make an adult human being.

The *Diary* Has Universal Appeal

Antony Kamm

The following article is a review of *Anne Frank: The Diary of a Young Girl* that appeared in 1994. For the reviewer, Antony Kamm, the *Diary* is the vehicle through which a teenager who wanted to be a writer found immortality. Kamm contends that, in the publication of her diary, Anne Frank simultaneously became a symbol of adolescent development under extraordinary circumstances and of the millions of Jews who did not survive the Holocaust.

In 1933 Otto Frank, the second son in a banking family, emigrated from Germany to Holland. He set up a business in Amsterdam selling pectin to housewives; eventually the business diversified into chemical and pharmaceutical products and herbs, particularly those used in the manufacture of sausages. He and his wife and two daughters lived in a modern apartment and had a wide circle of acquaintances, non-Jewish as well as Jewish, of whom many of the latter were members of the liberal Jewish community. On June 12, 1942, the younger daughter, Anne(liese), made the first entry in a diary which she had been given for her birthday. On July 9 the family went into hiding in the "Secret Annexe" constructed by Otto Frank in the building which his firm occupied, where they were joined by another family (of three) and a dentist.

A BOOK CALLED *HET ACHTERHUIS*

Anne continued her diary during their enforced incarceration. In March 1944, after listening to a radio broadcast about making a collection of diaries after the war, she had the idea of writing a "romance of the 'Secret Annexe.'" On May 11 she wrote: My greatest wish is to become a journal-

From Antony Kamm, "A Second Look: *Anne Frank: The Diary of a Young Girl*," *Horn Book Magazine*, November/December 1994. Reprinted by permission of The Horn Book, Inc., 11 Beacon St., Suite 1000, Boston, MA 02108.

ist someday and later on a famous writer.... In any case, I want to publish a book entitled *Het Achterhuis* [The Secret Annex] after the war. Whether I shall succeed or not, I cannot say, but my diary will be a great help.

On May 20, in a passage that was not included in the published diary, she wrote: "At long last after a great deal of reflection I have started my 'Achterhuis,' in my head it is as good as finished." She then began rewriting her original diary on loose sheets of paper, while keeping up regular entries in a notebook until the end of June and less regular ones in July; the last of all is dated August 1, 1944. On August 4, armed German police, accompanied by Dutch Nazis in plainclothes, raided the building and arrested the occupants of the office and the Annexe. The eight Jews were dispatched to concentration camps. Anne died of [typhus] in Bergen-Belsen in March 1945, a few days after her sister.

Anne's diaries and other manuscripts (including some stories) were left on the floor of the Annexe, having been tipped out of the briefcase in which she kept them by one of the policemen, who wanted a container for the money and jewelry which he had ordered the families to hand over at gunpoint. The manuscripts were preserved under lock and key and given to Otto Frank when he returned after the war; he was the only one of the eight inhabitants of the Secret Annexe who survived. In a form transcribed by him from the loose sheets and diary entries, Anne Frank's *Het Achterhuis* was published in Holland in 1947 and, as *The Diary of a Young Girl*... in England and the United States in 1952. Although written by a girl of fourteen, the book approximates what she herself intended to offer for publication rather than being simply a collection of diary entries for private consumption. (An article in *Het Parool* on April 3, 1946, stated that the Netherlands State Institute for War Documentation had acquired some two hundred of these private diaries.)

> I want to go on living even after my death! And therefore I am grateful to God for giving me this gift, this possibility of developing myself and of writing, of expressing all that is in me. (April 4, 1944)

A SYMBOL OF THE HOLOCAUST

That, through her diary, Anne Frank has become a symbol of the six million Jews murdered by the Nazis is due to a combination of circumstances. The novelist and critic Frederic Raphael has suggested that the appalling nature of the Holocaust is such that language is incapable of describing it. One of the survivors, Elie Wiesel, historian, novelist, and winner of the Nobel Peace Prize, stated in a *Paris Review* interview in 1978: "If I moved away from the theme of the Holocaust it was to protect it. I didn't want to abuse words; I didn't want to repeat words. I want to surround the subject with a fence of *kedushah*, of sacredness. To me the sanctuary of Jewish history is there; therefore I wrote other things in order not to write about that."

A FATHER'S DUTY

In 1979, the year before Otto Frank, Anne Frank's father, died, he talked about what Anne had wanted to do after the war and his duty to her.

Anne never spoke about hatred anywhere in her diary. She wrote that despite everything, she believed in the goodness of people. And that when the war was over, she wanted to work for the world and for people. This is the duty I have taken over from her. I have received many thousands of letters. Young people especially always want to know how these terrible things could ever have happened. I answer them as well as I can, and I often finish by saying: "I hope that Anne's book will have an effect on the rest of your life so that insofar as it is possible in your circumstances, you will work for unity and peace."

The Italian novelist and poet Primo Levi was preoccupied with the predicament of those, such as himself, who "felt innocent, yes, but enrolled among the saved and therefore in permanent search of a justification in my own eyes and those of others. The worst survived, that is, the fittest; the best all died." Anne Frank did not survive. It is the freshness as well as the innocence of her diary, cut off at the point beyond which life became unbearable, that have ensured its appeal to many who cannot bring themselves to read about or even contemplate what happened thereafter.

THE DEVELOPMENT OF A TEENAGER

By the end of the 1980s, nearly sixteen million copies had been sold worldwide. It has been and continues to be read by generations that were born and have grown up since the events it describes. *The Diary of a Young Girl* is, however, not only an extraordinary record of events which are rendered more immediate by the diary format and more dramatic by the unities of place and time imposed by the unnatural circumstances. It also reveals the uninhibited inner thoughts and feelings of an intelligent, articulate, self-critical teenager, and methodically and faithfully charts the development of her personality through various changes until she can say to her alter ego: I know what I want, I have a goal, an opinion. I have a religion and love. "Let me be myself and then I am satisfied. I know that I'm a woman, a woman with inward strength and plenty of courage." (April 11, 1944)

She has in the course of her unique exposition, as the poet and critic John Berryman pointed out, portrayed "the conversion of a child into a person."

In what she calls her "religion" lies a further key to the universal appeal of the diary. The Franks were not Orthodox Jews; they were assimilated Jews of liberal inclinations, as happy to celebrate Christmas with their gentile friends as Hanukkah with fellow Jews. Many young people today want to believe in God, without being shackled to a particular doctrine. Anne Frank, with her uncomplicated, universal brand of teenage theology, speaks for them, and to them.

Fifty years after Anne Frank finished her diary, it continues to speak to the young—and to all of us.

"I Believe in the Good Within Man"

Norbert Muhlen

Norbert Muhlen served as a foreign correspondent in Europe in the 1960s and is the author of several books, including *The Return of Germany.* In the article that follows, he speculates about Anne Frank's life had she survived World War II. Anne Frank, he explains, outlived her death to become a legend, revived by the force of the *Diary* and the effect her writing had on people after the trauma of the post-war years had lessened. He attributes the phenomenon to the universality of the themes that permeate her writing, including the development of a maturing adolescent and an inherent faith in the ultimate goodness of humanity.

If Anne Frank had not died at fifteen, she would now be twenty-nine years of age. One is tempted to speculate what this young woman would be today, had not a unique chain of events brought Hitler to power in her lifetime. Maybe she would be living as a wife and mother in the city of Frankfurt where her ancestors had lived for centuries—at ten, like other little girls of her age, she had voiced this ambition.

Or perhaps we would know her as a promising, if not famous, contemporary young writer. In her early teens, she often confided that she wanted to grow up to be an author. Before she was fourteen, she had already written a number of children's stories, with titles such as "The Flower Girl," "The Clever Dwarf," "The Bear Who Discovered the World." In their mixture of charming naiveté and surprisingly mature insights, these stories reveal the native talent of Anne as a story teller, her "enjoyment of being a fabulist," as Goethe called it.

Yet possibly she would have chosen a quite different vo-

Reprinted from Norbert Muhlen, "The Triumph of Anne Frank," *Commonweal,* October 31, 1958, by permission.

cation; those who knew her well said that she was "a little bundle of contradictions," and she herself wholeheartedly agreed with this characterization. We can only speculate; because her family was of Jewish descent, she was driven from her native country at four, forced to hide—self-immured in two small backrooms with her parents and her sister and four strangers—at thirteen and fourteen, and killed one year later, in a concentration camp.

THE REVIVAL OF ANNE FRANK

Yet her life on earth did not quite end then. Ten years after her death, she reappeared almost triumphantly in her native country and throughout the world. The children of those who had killed her, as well as the children of those who had been persecuted with her, came to love, and sometimes to revere, this revived Anne Frank.

The way of her revival was strange enough, and inspiring despite a touch of Broadway and best-seller business which served as its vehicle. When her father, the only one among the eight to survive, revisited the hideaway after Hitler's fall, he found the diary which she had written during her two years there [Actually, the diary was returned to Frank by the Dutch friends who had found and preserved it. *Ed.*] The document was published in Holland and shortly thereafter in a German translation.

The book received very little attention at the time. In those first post-war years, extremely few people in and out of Germany wanted to hear of "still another Nazi atrocity story," for reasons which varied with those who held them. Although Anne's *Diary* was by no means an atrocity story, the subject seemed already too remote to interest as "news," yet too close for a detached reading as history. By ignoring the book, people protected themselves against their still unhealed feelings of guilt—or of shame and mourning and helpless shock.

Only in 1952 was Anne Frank's *Diary* published in this country. A "successful" book, it was rendered into a play with great empathy and skill by the playwrights Frances [Goodrich] and Walter Hackett. The play was honored with a Pulitzer Prize. Only after these successes in America was Anne discovered by the Germans; and their response to her was sudden, spontaneous, powerful. A new generation unburdened by traumatic memories of the Hitler past had by now come of age. A new paperback edition of her *Diary* was followed by a German translation of the American play. The play, which opened on the German stage in the winter of 1956, has by now been presented in more than half of the legitimate theaters throughout West Germany, and with long runs. In these last years literally millions of Germans have encountered the person of Anne Frank.

As she became better known, the places in which she lived and died came to resemble shrines. The house on Prinsengracht in Amsterdam, where she wrote the *Diary*, has been turned in a pathetic Anne Frank Museum. Her birthplace in a residential Frankfurt street is honored by a plaque, and a memorial of fresh flowers, laid down every week by pious visitors, enlivens her burial place, in the former Belsen-Bergen concentration camp where she died of starvation [and typhus]. True, her burial place is merely a drab mound in the desolate North German Lueneburg Heath, and not even her name is inscribed; a sticker proclaims only that "20,000 are buried here." She disappeared among these anonymous gravemates who in turn disappear among Hitler's murdered millions—Jews, Germans, women, children, men of almost every nationality and faith.

A WILL TO LIVE

Why, then, was Anne Frank singled out from this mass, and what has she become in the eyes and hearts of the living who have brought her back to posthumous life? Anne Frank did not seem a very unusual girl, as we learn from the biography by Ernst Schnabel, a forty-five-year-old, able German Catholic writer. . . . In search of Anne, he tried to interview seventy-six people who had known her well, or whose paths had crossed hers; fifty of them are mentioned by Anne herself in her *Diary*. But by 1957 eighteen had died—only seven by natural deaths; others were missing or had left Europe. But he did succeed in finding forty-two people who told him what they remembered of Anne.

From these testimonies, which summon up a picture of her personality, the impression emerges that, as Herr Schnabel puts it, she was a child "like countless other children." None of his witnesses, with their fairly intimate and complete account of her life from nursery to the bitter end, claimed that she had been a *wunderkind*, or in any way unusual. "She was gracious, capricious at times, and full of ideas," Herr Schnabel sums up. "She had a tender, but also a critical spirit, a special gift for deep feelings and for fear, but also her own special kind of courage. . . ." As Anne's *Diary* ended before the worst began—whose fearful shadow, though, hovers ever-present over its pages—the reports on her way through the death camp add an important sequel to her own life story.

But here and there in these moving recollections appear glimpses of her more remarkable traits, such as, for instance, the compassion which led her to cry at the sight of fellow-victims while she herself had arrived at the worst suffering point; or her loneliness even before the persecution began—"I have several best friends, but no real friend," she once confided; and mainly, her admirable struggle to "keep face" in those death camp days of which one survivor said: "Do you think anyone in Belsen asked anyone else, 'Who are you?' Identity no longer existed there. There was only horror and confusion, and to be alive oneself was an almost superhuman effort." Anne tried to keep on living.

A MARTYR RATHER THAN A VICTIM

Of the reasons that have caused her strange return to the living, the first is obviously her unusual gift to observe the life around her and to think about her own life, and to write all this honestly and well. But what she saw, felt and put down in her *Diary* was much more than her own particular fate. Many young people, particularly in Germany, told me that Anne had captivated and conquered them because they could identify themselves with her and her problems, different though they may seem. They discovered the image of their own suffering and their own search for the good life in Anne's "extreme situation," as she lived and described it.

This extremity of a general human condition began with her immurement in a prison to which she had been sentenced without cause, to live there day and night with people who seemed to her sometimes ludicrous and sometimes lovable, often funny, mostly incomprehensible. If the Nazis robbed her of her freedom and threatened her life, she also felt that she was often misunderstood and mistreated by her fellow Jews in the hideout. But just as often she was puzzled, and sometimes shocked and agonized about herself when she discovered evil in her own nature. She was quite conscientious in repenting for what she felt were her sins, and often she was full of love and inner cheer. While she matured, her innocence began to give way to a search for "the sense of life" and for faith.

One sentence in her *Diary*, which serves as the motto of its German edition, has become a motto for many of her unorganized followers who range from Germany to Israel. "I believe," Anne Frank's *Credo* stated, "in the good within man." This she wrote after two years of suffering in her prison, with death nearby. As Herr Schnabel reports, one of his elderly interloculators who had also suffered much brushed it aside as proof of Anne's childishness. But I have heard young people—who knew nothing else about her—quote, discuss, uphold Anne's statement with enthusiasm.

If Anne Frank has become today the author of a posthumous best-seller, the heroine of a world-wide stage success and of a screenplay, she has also come to be—as a martyr rather than a victim—the image of a contemporary, secular legend. Ernst Schnabel's report seems to prove that while this legend corresponds quite accurately to the facts of her life, many see in it a meaning which transcends by far its individual, political or historical reality.

CHAPTER 2

Anne Frank and *The Diary of a Young Girl:* A Critical Assessment

The *Diary* Is Popular Because It Ignores Gritty Reality

Robert Alter

In her diary, Anne Frank deals candidly with the hopes and frustrations of her growing-up years. Readers tend to agree that in spite of the confinement she experiences and the turbulence and horror inflicted by the war raging outside her hiding place, Anne is a normal teenager who exhibits most of the characteristics and interests of just about any teenager of the time. In an article that includes a review of a new English version of the diary released in 1995—*The Diary of a Young Girl: The Definitive Edition*—American scholar and author Robert Alter attributes much of the popular attraction of the *Diary* to two factors. One is the absence of an adult perspective and "direct grappling with the barbarity of Nazism." Anne's perspective, in Alter's opinion, is one of "naive idealism," which is consistent with that of someone in his or her early teens . The other reason for the *Diary*'s wide appeal is its universalism. Anne's diary, Alter argues, is "a story of human interest, not a story about Jewish suffering."

More than half a century now separates us from the mass murders perpetrated by the Nazis, but judging by the continuing tide of historical studies, memoirs, novels and films, our collective fascination with the subject has grown with the passage of time. Historians have genuinely advanced understanding in numerous ways, but the popular imagination of the Nazi genocide continues to be caught between sensationalism and sentimentality. . . .

It is the second of these alternatives that is reflected in the persistent appeal of the Anne Frank story. The sad story of

From Robert Alter, "The View from the Attic," *New Republic,* December 4, 1995. Reprinted by permission of the *New Republic,* ©1995, The New Republic, Inc.

[Jewish-American author] Meyer Levin's obsession with *The Diary of Anne Frank* . . . is in most respects the peculiar story of one man's pathology. For all its peculiarity, however, it is also symptomatic in one regard of what our culture ever since the 1950s has sought to make of the destruction of European Jewry. . . .

In 1950, while living with his second wife, Tereska Torres, in the south of France, Levin came across Anne Frank's *Diary* in a French translation. He was profoundly moved. More than that, he became convinced . . . that through the *Diary* "the world could finally and clearly absorb the enormity of the mass murders perpetrated by the Nazis." It was, as I will suggest, an extravagant judgment, and it touches on the nexus between Levin's private obsession and the popular cult of Anne Frank that flourished in the '50s and still has not entirely faded. . . .

The new English version of *The Diary of a Young Girl* is based on a Dutch edition of 1991 that incorporated, for the first time, certain vitriolic comments by Anne about her fellow-tenants of the Secret Annex and reflections on her own nascent sexuality (including one fleeting impulse of adolescent lesbianism). Otto Frank [Anne's father], in the early aftermath of the war, had seen fit to delete these passages. The result of their inclusion is a more believable self-representation of Anne as a sometimes sharp-edged, touchy, lively girl. The new version is less sugar, more vinegar. And this is enhanced in Susan Massotty's translation, which, at least to judge by how it reads as English, nicely conveys the colloquial vivacity and spunkiness of the young diarist. Anne's estrangement from her mother, a familiar moment of female early adolescence, is more evident in the new version ("More than once, after a series of absurd reproaches, I've snapped at Mother: 'I don't care what you say. Why don't you wash your hands of me—I'm a hopeless case.'"). Her burgeoning literary self-consciousness as a diarist, writing and revising with an eye to eventual publication, is also now clearer.

A GENTLE TREATMENT OF THE HORRORS OF GENOCIDE

What is appealing about Anne Frank is the absolute teenage normalcy that she manifests in her diary. In fact, she registers the historical disaster around her only to the degree that it concretely compels her attention. The earliest entries, from the period before she goes into hiding with her family in July 1942, are full of anxious observations not about the Nazis but about school grades and promotion and friendships; the ominous German occupation is reflected only in her complaint about the inconvenience of being forbidden as a Jew to ride the streetcar. Once the family has taken refuge in the Secret Annex, Anne of course devotes space to the constant fear of detection, the physical hardships and what she hears of the course of the war. Even so, she concentrates largely on her relations with her parents and sis-

---

REST IN PEACE, ANNE

The following letter appears in Dear Anne Frank, *a collection of letters and extracts written in the 1990s by children and teens. The 15-year-old girl from Cleveland, Ohio, wrote the letter to tell Anne how she has inspired her and others.*

Dear Anne,

I feel I must write to you directly to explain my thoughts about your life. After all, that is what people truly celebrate when they read your diary. It is the sordid fact that you didn't make it which saddens people the most; it seems that all your optimism was for nothing. Although it may seem that it is your death which is remembered, I'd like to say to you that this is not the case. People feel inspired by your vivid mind and your will to live through bad times.

When I read your diary I feel as if I am living through it too. I believe that every one of your readers feels you should have lived.

The irony, of course, is that had you lived, your diary would most probably never have been published, at least until your eventual death.

That fact says to some people that your death wasn't totally in vain; something good came of it: that is, many people learned of the true horrors of the Holocaust. Maybe so, but that doesn't compensate in any way for the life of an intelligent, vibrant young girl. If you had lived, people would find out about the Holocaust in another way.

A memorial service was held on what would have been your sixty-fifth birthday. I read at that service. I felt that I was helping in a very small way to prevent another Holocaust.

I can imagine that many people in despair have read your diary and felt uplifted; it has given them the strength and inspiration to battle on.

Rest in peace. You deserve it, dear Anne.

ter and the other four hideouts, on her fluctuating infatua-
tion with one of them (Peter van Daan), on her developing
sense of self as an adolescent, on her sexual feelings and on
her literary ambitions. All this is humanly understandable
and perfectly natural, but how is it that Meyer Levin and so
many others could have seen it as a document through
which "the world could finally and clearly absorb the enormity of the mass murders perpetrated by the Nazis"?

Much of the popular attraction of the *Diary* derives, no
doubt, from the safe distance of indirection from the horrors
of genocide that it preserves for its readers. There are no
skeletal camp inmates, no gas chambers, no diabolical med-
ical experiments and acts of sadism. There is only the con-
cluding editorial note that after the S.S. arrested the eight
tenants of the Secret Annex on August 4, 1944, and their deportation to the death-camps, only Otto Frank survived. And
so I am tempted to say that the widespread disposition to
take the *Diary* as the emblematic testimony of the murdered
6 million betrays a failure of moral imagination—as though
without it we could not imagine concretely that there were
countless young girls and boys (not to speak of the adults
and the old people) with hopes and dreams for a personal
future who were torn from life before they could really begin
to live it.

I do not mean to sound impervious to the poignancy of the
Diary. Still, many diaries of Jews who perished have been
published that reflect a complexity of adult perspective and,
in some instances, a direct grappling with the barbarity of
Nazism; and these are absent from Anne Frank's writing.
For this reason, the emblematic power attributed to her book
seems a little odd. I suspect it can be explained by two traits
of the diarist: her adolescence and the marginal nature of
her Jewish identity. . . .

ANNE'S DEATH HELPS THE DIARY ENDURE

Precisely because the writer is in her early teens, *The Diary
of a Young Girl* provides just the sort of feel-sad, feel-good
representation of genocide that American audiences (and, to
a large extent, European audiences) were looking for in the
1950s. Anne may have been a bright and admirably intro-
spective girl, but there is not much in her diary that is emo-
tionally demanding, and her reflections on the world have
the quality of banality that one would expect from a 14-year-

old. What makes the *Diary* moving is the shadow cast back over it by the notice of her death at the end. Try to imagine . . . an Anne Frank who survived Bergen-Belsen, and, let us say, settled in Cleveland, became a journalist, married and had two children. Would anyone care about her wartime diary except as an account of the material circumstances of hiding out from the Nazis in Amsterdam?

Looking out from an attic window over the rooftops of Amsterdam, Anne reflects: "As long as this exists, this sunshine and this cloudless sky, and as long as I can enjoy it, how can I be sad?" Elsewhere, thinking about the kind of person she is, she writes: "I'm happy, and I intend to stay that way! I was born happy, I love people, and I have a trusting nature, and I'd like everyone else to be happy too." And in the most famous of these affirmations, in one of her last entries, . . . she acclaims: "I still believe, in spite of everything, that people are good at heart." There is a kind of fortuitous complicity, I think, between these understandably sentimental simplifications of a young girl's naive idealism and the ersatz idealism that is the stock-in-trade of Broadway and Hollywood and the publishing industry. . . .

Though there is surely something to be said for a document that enables us to identify imaginatively with a victim of these terrible events, the adolescent Anne may too readily inspire sympathy of an adolescent sort. Recently I came across an unforgettable example. The popular novelist Pat Conroy confessed to the Foreword that he "fell in love" with Anne Frank when his mother first read him the *Diary* as a child, and he added: "In the book there are these little pictures and Anne looks so nice, her dark eyes smiling. . . . I used to imagine, if only I'd been in the attic with Anne, instead of that boy who obviously didn't cut the mustard with her. I could have helped her have more fun."

THE JEWISHNESS OF ANNE

The other chief source of the *Diary*'s wide appeal is its anodyne universalism. Otto Frank repeatedly insisted that his daughter's diary was a story of general human interest, not a story about Jewish suffering, and with only minor qualifications I think that he was right. Anne is acutely aware, of course, that her life is threatened because she is a Jew, and even before she went into hiding, Nazi regulations obliged her to attend a Jewish secondary school. The Franks were in no way self-denying or self-hating Jews, but they were thoroughly acculturated as Western Europeans.

For Anne, however, being a Jew is like being freckled or being left-handed. It has no specific content or deep resonance. Historical circumstances had turned it into a grave liability, as would be the case for a left-handed person under a regime that suddenly declared all such sinister deviants were to be rounded up for extermination. . . .

There are references to the Jews in the *Diary*, but they are few and far between. Moreover, Anne is ambivalent about whether she really wants to embrace the idea of being a Jew or transcend it. Characteristically, in a late entry, she first says, "We've been strongly reminded of the fact that we're Jews in chains, chained to one spot, without any rights," and she looks forward to a time after the war "when we'll be people again and not just Jews!" But then she swings in the opposite direction and wonders whether someday the experience of suffering will make the Jews moral exemplars, "And we'll have to keep on being Jews, but then, we'll want to be." Anne's universalizing bent reflects a continuity of values with her father, who labored to rescue her legacy from the claims of Jewish particularism. The Anne Frank Foundation, which he helped to establish in 1957, declared that its principal purpose "would be to use the name of Anne Frank as a symbol for all constructive activity relating in any way to adolescents . . . , which furthers inter-group understanding in an atmosphere of freedom and hope.". . .

The *Diary* . . . includes only a glancing reference to [the celebration of Hanukkah in the Secret Annex] (it is the sole Jewish ritual mentioned). . . . Otto Frank had wanted his daughter to be given a Bible for Hanukkah "so I could finally learn something about the New Testament." Both Anne and her sister wondered about the appropriateness of the holiday for the gift, and their father conceded that "Well, maybe St. Nicholas Day would be a better occasion." There is nothing inherently wrong, of course, with Anne Frank's being a residual Jew, and it is horrifying that an ideology of racial hatred should have turned that residue into a death-sentence. Still, it is impossible to "universalize" a document that is already universal.

The fact that she was neither very Jewish nor very mature has neatly suited the purposes of a sanitized, homey, uplifting version of Germany's pathological onslaught on the Jewish people. *The Diary of a Young Girl* does not trouble readers with the bothersome presence of a Jewish people nurturing its various senses of collective identity and its various but distinctive traditions, and singled out for destruction because it is perceived by the murderers as an inassimilable collective Other. The bland message . . . that we are all victims at one time or another . . . is really not very far from Anne's way of seeing things. At the same time, the innocent, uncomplicated idealism of her sense of life as a 14-year-old has been reassuring for millions of readers who prefer not to examine too closely the ugly concreteness of historical evil, or to contemplate the terrible possibility that it may go on and on.

Anne Frank invites us to look at the sunshine and the cloudless sky and the resilient goodness of the spirit of man. Considering what the spirit of man perpetrated from 1933 to 1945, and has perpetrated since, I wonder if that is where we really need to look.

Anne Frank Has Been Denied Her Place as a Mature Woman Writer

Catherine A. Bernard

Catherine A. Bernard wrote the following article about Anne Frank as part of her thesis on female writers of the Holocaust. Bernard considers Anne Frank the "best and least known of the female documentors of Nazi terror." Her thesis provides insight into the different editions of Anne Frank's *Diary* and into how they have been interpreted. Bernard argues that Anne's diary has continually been edited to relegate her to the role of inspirational victim instead of according her the recognition she deserves as an insightful and talented female writer.

On May 5, 1985, a few hours before his infamous visit with [German] Chancellor Helmut Kohl to the German cemetery at Bitburg, U.S. President Ronald Reagan addressed a crowd at the former concentration camp of Bergen-Belsen. As he commemorated the thirty thousand victims of Bergen-Belsen, Reagan sought to ameliorate the atmosphere of death and despair by invoking the name of Anne Frank:

> And too many of them knew that this was their fate. But that was not the end. Through it all was their faith and a spirit that moved their faith.

> Nothing illustrates this better than the story of a young girl who died here at Bergen-Belsen. For more than two years, Anne Frank and her family had hidden from the Nazis in a confined annex in Holland, where she kept a remarkably profound diary. Betrayed by an informant, Anne and her family were sent by freight car to Auschwitz and finally here to Bergen-Belsen.

> Just three weeks before her capture, young Anne wrote these words: "It's really a wonder that I haven't dropped all ideals,

From Catherine A. Bernard, "Anne Frank: The Cultivation of the Inspirational Victim," part 4 of "tell him that I . . . Women Writing the Holocaust," *Modern Thought and Literature*, Winter 1995, pp. 37–56. Reprinted by permission of the author.

because they seem so absurd and impossible to carry out. Yet I keep them, because in spite of everything I still believe that people are really good at heart. I simply can't build up my hopes on a foundation consisting of confusion, misery, and death. I see the world gradually being turned into a wilderness, I hear the ever approaching thunder, which will destroy us too, I can feel the suffering of millions, and yet, if I look up into the heavens, I think that it will all come right, that this cruelty, too, will end, and that peace and tranquillity will reign again."

Eight months later, this sparkling young life ended at Bergen-Belsen.

Somewhere here lies Anne Frank. Everywhere here are memories—pulling us, touching us, making us understand that they can never be erased. Such memories take us where God intended his children to go—toward learning, toward healing, and, above all, toward redemption. They beckon us through the endless stretch of our heart to the knowing commitment that the life of each individual can change the world and make it better.

Anne Frank is simultaneously the best and the least known of the female documentors of Nazi terror. Her diary has been translated into numerous languages and is part of the curriculum in schools around the world; yet despite her embrace by this general audience, she has been for the most part gently but unambiguously dismissed as a figure not meriting serious academic examination. Therefore, although her name earns a level of recognition matched by few if any survivors of the Holocaust, little effort has been expended in analyzing her voice. Hers remains a life largely unexamined, except by her own self. . . .

ANNE THE FEMINIST

[Themes identified] as female-centered—anatomy and destiny—resonate throughout Frank's diary as Anne meditates on her relationship with her mother, on her emerging sexuality, and on the status of women in her culture, and would therefore seem to have quite a bit to do with the concerns of women in the camps, especially since many of the women in the camps had very recently been adolescents just like Anne. . . .

It has been terribly important to isolate Anne from the impurity of adulthood in order to facilitate her function as a redemptive figure, to provide a point of uplift in what would otherwise be, after all, an unremittingly depressing historical event. The above speech by Reagan is an example of the means by which Frank, whose force putatively comes from her identity as a historical figure, has been emptied of her particularity and nudged into a ... role as both a palatable and a forgiving representative of the victims of fascism. Consequently, any desire to examine the *Diary of Anne Frank* as the complex expression of an actual young woman has been far eclipsed by the importance of maintaining Frank's symbolic role as the ultimate innocent victim. And foremost, apparently, that maintenance has taken the form of eliminating reference to both Anne's femaleness and to her emerging sexuality.

Most of those familiar with Anne Frank would, like Reagan, be able to parrot the oft-quoted phrase "I still believe that people are really good at heart." But few would recognize the following as a conviction argued with equal fortitude by Anne:

> A question that has been raised more than once and that gives me no inner peace is why did so many nations in the past, and often still now, treat women as inferior to men? Everyone can agree how unjust this is, but that is not enough for me, I would also like to know the cause of the great injustice!

> Presumably man, thanks to his greater physical strength, achieved dominance over woman from the very start; man, who earns the money, who begets children, who may do what he wants. ... It is stupid enough of women to have borne it all in silence for such a long time, since the more centuries this arrangement lasts, the more deeply rooted it becomes. Luckily schooling, work and progress have opened women's eyes. In many countries, women have been granted equal rights; many people, particularly women, but also men, now realize for how long this state of affairs has been wrong, and modern women demand the right of complete independence!

> But that's not all, respect for woman, that's going to have to come as well! Generally, man is held in high esteem all over the world; why shouldn't women have a share in this? Soldiers and war heroes are honored and celebrated, explorers acquire immortal fame, martyrs are revered, but how many will look upon woman as they would upon a soldier?

> There is something in the book "The Fight for Life" that has affected me deeply, along the lines that women suffer more pain, more illness and more misery than any war hero just from giving birth to children. And what reward does woman reap for coming successfully through all this pain? She is pushed to one side should she lose her figure through giving birth, her children soon leave her, her beauty passes. Women are much braver, much more courageous soldiers, struggling

and enduring pain for the continuance of mankind, than all the freedom-fighting heroes with their big mouths!

In no way do I mean by this that women should turn against childbearing, on the contrary, nature has made them like that and that is all to the good. I merely condemn all the men, and the whole system, that refuse ever to acknowledge what an important, arduous, and in the long run beautiful part women play in society.

I fully agree with Paul de Kruif, the author of the above-mentioned book, when he says that men must learn that birth has ceased to mean something natural and ordinary in those parts of the world we consider civilized. It's very easy for men to talk, they don't and will never have to bear the miseries of women!

I believe that the idea that a woman's duty is simply to bear children will change over the centuries to come and will make way for respect and admiration for one who without complaint and a lot of talk shoulders all these burdens!

yours, Anne M. Frank.

The above should be completely unfamiliar to anyone who has ever read the American edition of *Diary of a Young Girl*, and for good reason: although written by Anne on June 15, 1944, only two weeks before her final entry, it was deleted from the original Dutch edition and therefore from its translations, although the rest of the entry of which it was part was retained. The reasons for this are entirely unclear, unless one accepts that for some reason these very adult and feminist statements were somehow seen as incompatible with the purpose of the book, or unacceptable to the reading public. Not until 1986, when the critical edition of the diary was published in Holland (the English translation appeared in 1989), was this passage available. . . .

WRITING AND EDITING THE DIARY

The critical edition also for the first time revealed vital facts about the diary: that Anne herself, a few months before her capture, had begun to edit her diary herself in preparation for publication after the war, and that the version published in 1947 had been redacted from the originals and from Anne's partially completed manuscript, with sometimes extensive editing not only by Otto Frank, her father, but also by his colleagues and, in some cases, by translators. In many cases, deletions in the published version followed deletions Anne herself had indicated, but in some cases, often signifi-

cantly, they did not. It is unlikely, for example, upon review-
ing the nature of Anne's own deletions, which were mostly
items which were overly personal or petty, such as negative
remarks about her classmates written when she was thirteen, that she would not have retained the above passage, especially since she wrote it concurrently with her editing.

Anne Frank began to edit her diary in response to an address on March 28, 1944, by exiled Minister of Education,
Art and Science Gerrit Bolkstein, delivered to the Dutch nation on Radio Oranje:

> History cannot be written on the basis of official decisions
> and documents alone. If our descendants are to understand
> fully what we as a nation have had to endure and overcome
> during these years, then what we really need are ordinary
> documents—a diary, letters from a worker in Germany, a col-
> lection of sermons given by a parson or a priest. Not until we
> succeed in bringing together vast quantities of this simple,
> everyday material will the picture of our struggle for freedom
> be painted in its full depth and glory.

The next day, Anne wrote, "Of course, they all made a
rush at my diary immediately. . . . Just imagine how interesting it would be if I were to publish a romance of the 'Secret
Annexe.' The title alone would be enough to make people
think it was a detective story." By May 11, her consideration
of the idea had taken on a much more serious tone, and she
wrote that:

> You've known for a long time that my greatest wish is to be-
> come a journalist someday and later on a famous writer.
> Whether these leanings towards greatness (or insanity?) will
> ever materialize remains to be seen, but I certainly have the
> subjects in my mind. In any case, I want to publish a book en-
> titled *Het Achterhuis* after the war. Whether I shall succeed or
> not I cannot say, but my diary will be a great help.

And finally, in a remark also deleted from previous published versions of the diary, she wrote on May 20 that "after
a good deal of reflection I have started my 'Achterhuis,' in my
head it is as good as finished, although it won't go as quickly
as that really, if it ever comes off at all." We may assume that
subsequent entries were made with the idea of publication
in mind, and that therefore that the entry of June 15, with all
its passion and vitality, would be one Anne would have
wanted included. . . .

At this point, some information on the diary's publication
history and on its initial critical reception may serve to begin

to answer the questions which have been raised. The diary had been abandoned when the Franks' Secret Annexe was raided, on August 4, 1944, and was rescued and hidden by Miep Gies. Gies actually recovered three separate exercise books and some loose sheets, containing Anne's entries from her thirteenth birthday in June of 1942 up to her last entry on August 1, 1944. Approximately a year later, after Otto Frank, Anne's father and the only surviving member of the family, had returned to Amsterdam, Gies handed Anne's writings over to him. He immediately began to edit the diaries into a single typescript and to seek out a publisher. As mentioned, Otto Frank did not merely copy out the diaries; he edited out items which he felt were offensive to his dead wife or to other third parties, as well as items which he "felt would be of little interest," a point which begs clarification.

Frank was unsuccessful in finding a publisher until, in 1946, the eminent Dutch historian Jan Romein read the manuscript and wrote an article about it in the journal *Het Parool*, entitled "A Child's Voice":

> By chance a diary written during the war years has come into my possession. The Netherlands State Institute for War Documentation already holds some two hundred similar diaries, but I should be very much surprised if there were another one as lucid, as intelligent, and at the same time as natural....
>
> The way [Anne Frank] died is in any case not important. What matters far more is that her young life was willfully cut short by a system whose witless barbarity we swore never to forget or forgive while it still raged, but which, now that it belongs to the past, we are already busily, if not forgiving, then forgetting, which ultimately comes to the same thing.
>
> To me, however, this apparently unconsequential [sic] diary, this "de profundis" stammered out in a child's voice, embodies all the hideousness of fascism, more so than all the evidence of Nuremberg put together. To me the fate of this Jewish girl epitomizes the worst crime perpetrated by everlastingly abominable minds. For the worst crime is not the destruction of life and culture as such—these could also fall victim to a culture-creating revolution—but the throttling of the sources of culture, the destruction of life and talent for the mere sake of mindless destructiveness....
>
> That this girl could have been abducted and murdered proves to me that we have lost the fight against human bestiality.

It is not surprising that shortly afterward, Frank was besieged by publishers, and that the Dutch edition of the diary, entitled, as Anne had wished, *Het Achterhuis* ("The Attic/

Secret Annexe"), published by the Dutch house Contact, appeared a year later. . . .

INTERPRETING THE MESSAGE OF THE *DIARY*

Very rapidly, however, it would be established that the message of the *Diary* was one far different than that with which Romein had identified. This is expressed quite perfectly by the reviewers who glowingly orated that *Het Achterhuis* was "a miracle," "uniquely tragic," and "transcends the misery so recently [in 1947] behind us"; it was a "moral testament" and "a human document of great clarity and honesty," and, it was stressed, "by no means a war document as such [but] . . . purely and simply the diary of an adolescent girl." Whereas Romein could not but meditate on the murder of Anne Frank, his colleague Henri van Praag suggested that Frank should be viewed as a figure which exhorted the ideals of a moral life. . . .

What happened, in short, is that the tortured reading which Romein had gleaned from the diary was soon entirely replaced by the popular conception of the *Diary of Anne Frank* as an inspirational text. This interpretation, despite the periodic appearance of some excellent challenges, has held to this day. Anne herself was transformed into an empty vessel, and her voice glorified as pure, innocent, completely unblemished. To read the forewords which accompanied the first translated editions—*The Diary of a Young Girl* in English, *Das Tagebuch der Anne Frank* in German, *Journal de Anne Frank* in French—is to begin to understand the function of this consecrated and inviolate Anne; in each foreword she is made to serve for each nation as a flattering mirror-image of itself. To Eleanor Roosevelt, this young girl, "not afraid of telling the truth," is a symbol of American pluck; for the triumphant, always unconventional French, her unusual and spirited observations defy all that is "dusty and discolored"; for the wary and weary Germans, Anne's "cool, keen observation of human beings, and her resolve to be alert to the comic element in even the worst situations, these are familiar to us: they belong to the armor worn by our generation." Thus, stripped and reassembled, Anne was to serve as a redemptive figure for the suffering masses, an assurance that despite the evidence of the Holocaust, humanity was fundamentally good, that the devastation wreaked by the Nazis had been but a momentary lapse in the ultimate civilizing trajectory of Western culture....

The 1955 stage play by Francis Goodrich and Albert Hackett and the film version of the play released in 1959 were instrumental in interpreting Anne's writings according to a universalist ethic. The public perception of the writings of Anne Frank has been shaped as much by the enormously successful play and movie versions of the diary as by the diary itself, and perhaps more so. Even [psychoanalyst Bruno] Bettelheim notes that his objections are based not on "what actually happened to the Frank family—only on the account given in Anne's *Diary* and in the play and movie based on it," neglecting to distinguish between the degree of accuracy manifested by a historical document and by its fictionalizations. The adaptations of the diary differ significantly from their source in terms of focus and characterization. Meyer Levin, who sued after his own stage adaptation was rejected by Otto Frank, describes bitterly in his aptly-titled memoir *The Obsession* how Anne's musings were emptied of their Jewish particularity in order to guarantee their appeal to a gentile audience. Judith E. Doneson contends that this was done in accordance with the assimilationist ideals of the 1950's, and that, ironically, it resulted in simplified characters which contributed, if unintentionally, to conventional anti-Semitic stereotypes of the inhabitants of the Secret Annexe as nervous, weak Jews at the mercy of their courageous Christian friends. The exception, of course, is Anne herself, whose strong awareness of herself as a Jew and a woman is replaced by an irrepressibly optimistic and entirely lovable childlike figure whose triumphant final declaration—that, of course, she still believes people good at heart—banishes the feelings of horror and fright which might have overcome the audience upon learning of her cruel end. That this line "does not appear in the diary in anything like the climactic role it is made to assume in the play," and that "As Lawrence Langer has written, this line, 'floating over the audience like a benediction assuring grace after momentary gloom, is the least appropriate epitaph conceivable for the millions of victims and thousands of survivors of Nazi genocide,'" has not altered the tendencies of enormously influential speechifiers such as Reagan. It is useless to point out that Anne wrote these words long before she experienced Auschwitz....

ANNE FRANK AS A WOMAN WRITER

Berteke Waaldijk is one of the first scholars to question the degree to which Anne's specific identity as a woman has been underrepresented. She focuses in part on the differences between the three versions of the diary—the unabridged, that containing Anne's own revisions, and that finally published—and finds that "Although the differences may be negligible from the point of view of the political and judicial claims of authenticity," in the face of which the critical edition had in fact been compiled, "they are extremely significant for readers interested in Anne Frank as a woman writer." Waaldijk finds that in most cases, the passages removed dealt directly with aspects of Anne's experiences as a woman: "They have to do with her body, menstruation and sexuality, her conversations with Peter about sex, and her relationship with her mother." The remarks Anne had made about her mother were deleted by Otto Frank exclusively. Waaldijk claims that within the diary these observations were generally a manifestation of Anne's normal adolescent rebellion from her mother; the separation Anne desired could not be physically achieved while her family was in hiding, and she compensated by articulating, sometimes harshly, a mental distance from her mother. That Otto Frank, so shortly after the murder of his wife, could not tolerate the publication of these passages is understandable. Yet in censoring Anne's complex relationship with her mother, he also undoubtedly removed an important part of her. Various passages concerning Anne's sexuality, however, were deleted by both Anne and her father. For example, Anne chose to leave out of her rewritten version a one-page description of her genitals. "Because Anne Frank never finished her editing," Waaldijk explains, "we cannot be sure that would not have resurfaced in some other form, but it would clearly be wrong to picture her only as the object of silencing."

The difference, however, between the nature of the elimination of Anne's sexuality from the popular portrayals of her diary and Anne's own self-censorship is this: whereas overt references to Anne's sexuality were eliminated . . . because they were felt to be offensive and because they interfered with the stylization of Anne as the ultimate childlike innocent, Anne removed passages because she felt they made her appear immature. A passage composed on October 22, 1942, in which thirteen-year-old Anne expresses her impatience for the onset of menarche, was deleted in both Anne's and the published version, and in a note to the page penned on January 22, 1944, Anne writes, in a tone of embarrassed dismay, "I shall never be able to write such things again!" She takes advantage, that same day, of a page she had left blank in her first diary to elaborate:

> It was stupid of me to have left all these lovely pages blank, but perhaps it'll be all to the good if I am now able to put down my thoughts in general about what I have written. When I look over my diary today, 1½ years on, I cannot believe that I was ever such an innocent young thing. I cannot help but realize that no matter how much I should like to, I can never be like that again. I still understand those moods, those remarks about Margot, Mummy and Daddy so well that I might have written them yesterday, but I no longer understand how I could write so freely about other things.
>
> I really blush with shame when I read the pages dealing with subjects that I'd much better have left to the imagination. I put it all down so bluntly! But enough of that.

Anne ultimately deleted these two notes to herself as well, as did her father. What controversy there has been about the diary has been centered, in fact, upon Anne's descriptions of her emerging sexuality. As recently as 1982, the book was challenged in a Virginia school by parents who complained that the book was offensive due to its sexual content. And to Ditlieb Felderer, whose tract *Anne Frank's Diary—A Hoax* was one of the challenges to the diary's authenticity (and by extension to the historicity of the Holocaust itself) which the critical edition was published to answer, both the mature nature of Anne's writing and the mere existence of her sexuality were cause for doubt:

> At the end [of the official Anne Frank Foundation Amsterdam brochure], we are finally shown an excerpt purporting to belong to Anne Frank, then 15 years old. Somehow this excerpt, the only one given in the brochure, does not fit our conception of a girl at that age. [The passage to which Ditlieb refers is that quoted by Reagan above.]

Another matter which strikes the reader is that the diary is not the type of story one would want one's own child to write. It is not a KIND story. It is not the sign of a healthy child. Indeed it leaves the air of being a product of someone who tries to invent a child's mind but is unable to do so, sprinkling it with "sexy" portions to sell the story.... We cannot make out why a girl living under these circumstances would be preoccupied with all these "love affairs" at such tender age. In today's promiscuous society it may be an ordinary thing but not during the war.... Apparently the "sexy" portions were too much even for some Jews to stomach, and one of the first, if not the only group, to voice their objections against the diary, were some Orthodox Jews who felt it gave the Jews a bad image. A proper girl would not act in such a way. Whether their objections were based on true moral grounds or for fear that the story was letting the cat out of the bag may be debatable. Talmudic sources are certainly not foreign to perverse sex.

ANTI-GERMAN SENTIMENT IN THE DIARY

Upon first glance, the blatant antisemitism of revisionists ... may seem to have no connection with the adoration most express for Anne Frank. Yet the hateful intolerance of one finds a friend, unfortunately, in the self-protective blindness of the other.... In the critical edition, editor Gerrold van der Stroom remarks at length on the degree to which the German translator, Anneliese Schutz, took it upon herself to edit out some of Anne's more anti-German sentiments:

> The explanation that to those listening to the radio in the Annexe "there were no forbidden stations with the proviso that it was understood that only exceptionally could one listen to German stations, for instance to hear classical music and the like," was omitted from the German version.... The Dutch: "And indeed, there is no greater hostility than exists between Germans and Jews," became in German: "And there is no greater hostility in the world than between these Germans and Jews!"... The rule that people in the Annexe were required "to speak softly at all times, in any civilized language, therefore not in German," became in translation: "Alle Kultursprachen ... aber leise!!! [All civilized languages ... but softly!!!]."

Alvin H. Rosenfeld informs us that Goodrich and Hackett took pains to minimize, in their adaptation, Anne's very understandable animosity towards the Germans:

> Peering out of her hideaway windows, for instance, Anne Frank saw and recorded the brutality of the German occupation (entry of November 19, 1942):

>> Evening after evening the green and gray army lorries trundle past. The Germans ring at every front door to inquire if there are any Jews living in the house. If there are, then the whole family has to go at once. If they don't find any, they go on to the next house. No one has a chance of evading them

unless one goes into hiding. . . . It seems like the slave hunts of olden times. But it's certainly no joke; it's much too tragic for that. In the evenings when it's dark, I often see rows of good innocent people accompanied by crying children, walking on and on . . . bullied and knocked about until they almost drop. No one is spared—old people, babies, expectant mothers, the sick—each and all join in the march of death.

. . . no such passage as the one just quoted appears in the stage play.

Indeed, no such passage appears in either the play or the film; it would be fundamentally at odds with the "indestructibly affirmative" Anne which they labored to create. And this inability to cope with Anne's complexity marks a reluctance to face both the questions she posed and the answers suggested by her fate. . . .

THE REAL ANNE

To sum, the suppression of different aspects of the real Anne Frank facilitated, and in fact may have been necessary in, her transformation into an idealized figure who served to sweeten the bitter cup of the *Shoah* [the Holocaust]. In deleting the details pertaining to Anne's complex relationship with her mother, to her sexual awakening, and to her anger towards the misogyny of her society, many of the references to Anne's womanhood were lost; this made it all the easier to relegate Anne Frank to the easily manipulable role of a child. Anne's bitter sense of the fate the Nazis had designed for her and her drive to become a writer, expressed with force and fluency, pointed to a mind which had been disillusioned and which longed to describe the world in its own terms: many of these observations, too, were altered or deleted, permitting "the reduction of Anne Frank to a symbol of moral and intellectual convenience," to a mechanism for easy forgiveness.

It is highly ironic that the public has been prevented from knowing Anne as a woman or as a mature writer, because she saw these two aspects of herself as intricately related. The rejection of her mother and of her mother's role as a bourgeois housewife was deeply linked to Anne's literary ambitions. As Waaldijk explains, and as is evident in the entry of April 4, 1944 quoted below, "Anne's wish to lead the life of a writer coincides with her desire to lead a better life than that of her mother":

And now it's all over. I must work, so as not to be a fool, to get on, to become a journalist, because that's what I want! I know that I can write, a couple of my stories are good, my descriptions of the "Secret Annexe" are humorous, there's a lot in my diary that speaks, but—whether I have real talent remains to be seen.

I am the best and sharpest critic of my own work, I know myself what is and is not well written. Anyone who doesn't write doesn't know how wonderful it is . . .

And if I haven't any talent for writing books or newspaper articles, well, then I can always write for myself. But I want to get on; I can't imagine that I would have to lead the same sort of life as Mummy and Mrs. v.P. and all the women who do their work and are then forgotten, I must have something besides a husband and children, something that I can devote myself to!

I want to go on living even after my death! And therefore I am grateful to God for giving me this gift, this possibility of developing myself and of writing, of expressing all that is in me!

The question remains to what extent the popularization and valorization of Anne Frank has had an impact on other women writers of the Holocaust. Anne Frank was and continues to be blatantly denied status as a woman; this coincides disquietingly with the pressure to omit or minimize the importance of the question of gender in critical works about the Holocaust, and suggests that Anne Frank may have left behind a legacy with which she would not be content. In addition, one must wonder whether the enormous critical and commercial success of Anne Frank's diary has had anything to do with the fact that the majority of women's literary contributions to the subject are in the form of diaries or memoirs. The diary, after all, seems to be a perfect expression of the role to which women have been relegated time and time again: it is personal, emotional, unobtrusive, spontaneous and without "serious" literary pretensions. Anne Frank ventured far outside these guidelines, but she was posthumously forced back into them.

Anne Frank's *Diary* Remains a Searing Document of the Holocaust

Sara Laschever

Sara Laschever is the executive editor of *millennium pop*. She has written articles for the *New York Times*, the *Village Voice*, the *New York Times Book Review*, and other publications.
In this review of *The Diary of a Young Girl: The Definitive Edition*, Laschever compares Anne Frank to her own mother, a Jewish journalist born the same year as Frank. She uses the comparison as a basis for her belief in Anne Frank's "remarkable modernity." The contemporary feel of the *Diary* causes Anne to emerge as more than a feminist of her generation. Her diary creates a world unto itself, a world that is all too real despite the fact that it omits the harshest truths of the fate of Anne Frank herself. This fires the belief of some readers and critics that the *Diary* has been used to blunt the reality of the Holocaust as much as it has been used to keep alive the memories of the atrocities associated with it.

Anne Frank could have been my mother. By that I don't mean that my mother was a German Jewish teenager who hid from the Nazis in Holland during the war. Nor do I mean that every Jew born since the Holocaust is a child of the generation that endured it, although I think that this is true. What I mean is much more literal and personal: Anne Frank could have been my mother. Born barely a year apart (my mother in 1928 and Anne Frank in 1929) to middle-class Jewish families, both girls enjoyed sheltered '30s childhoods. And both of them—bright, cosseted daughters of dot-

From Sara Laschever, "World of Our Mothers: The Persistence of Anne Frank," first published in *millennium pop*, vol. 2, issue 2, Spring 1995. Reprinted with permission.

ing parents—conceived a strong desire to shape their lives very differently from those of their own mothers. "One of the many questions that have often bothered me is why women have been, and still are, thought to be so inferior to men," Anne wrote. Casting her lot with "modern women" who "want the right to be completely independent," she resolved: "If God lets me live, I'll achieve more than Mother ever did." She wanted a larger sphere of action than her mother's wholly domestic life could provide. She wanted a career, she wanted to be famous, and she wanted to be remembered after she was dead. She loved to write, and decided to be a journalist. My mother, though in a position to take her pick of the eligible young Jewish bachelors in Buffalo, New York (where she grew up), also decided at about the same age to become a journalist. The difference is that today, at 67, my mother is still a working journalist, having spent her life doing the work she loves, and Anne Frank is 50 years dead, and the author of one of the most famous books in the world.

My point in recounting these similarities is not simply to highlight the injustice of Anne Frank's fate, or to speciously identify myself with a beloved icon. My point is to note Anne Frank's remarkable modernity. Reading the new, expanded version of her diary . . . , one is struck first by how contemporary she is, how familiar her concerns, her view of her life and her world sound even five decades later. She was born into a generation of women that helped transform life in the Western world in the second half of this century, and rereading her reminds us that Betty Friedan did not leap fully formed out of the Eisenhower '50s. Though they weren't necessarily activists, the generation of young women who lived through World War II—the teenagers and college students, the WAVEs and WACs and WASPs and Rosie the Riveters—laid the groundwork for the women who came after them. By the 1970s, when the Women's Movement was calling into question a whole host of received ideas about women's roles and capabilities, my mother, like thousands of these women in Europe and America, had been pursuing her profession, with only a brief hiatus to get four children born and into kindergarten, for over 20 years.

THE PHENOMENON OF THE DIARY

The contemporary-seeming qualities of Anne's diary make her more than just another mother of modern feminism, however. They help explain the enduring power and popularity of her diary, which by some reckonings has been read by more people around the world than any other book besides the Bible. . . . Her wholly recognizable sensibility obliterates the safe distance we build between ourselves and previous generations. It makes it impossible for us to view the Frank family and the other people hiding in the Secret Annex as simply, in [the poet] Philip Larkin's famous phrase, "fools in old-style hats and coats."

Anne makes her experience of the Holocaust more real than any hundred histories, movies, or museums. She makes it impossible for us to retreat behind a lack of identification with the victims—all those luckless hordes captured in black-and-white photographs with their strange-looking beards, their hooded and private faces. Still, this alone could not make the diary the ongoing phenomenon it has become. Most of us will avoid facing the full extent of man's capacity for cruelty and carnage, if we can. If we admitted the truth of how dangerous the people around us might be, functioning from day to day could become impossible. Motivated by a sense of debt to the dead or by other compunctions, a certain kind of reader will seek out books that convey the harsh realities of the past. But unless those books have prurient or sensationalistic elements, they will probably not have enough readers to make them bestsellers, much less propel them into the ranks of the best-selling books of all time.

And Anne Frank's diary is not remotely prurient or sensational. What it is, instead, is enjoyable. It's fun to read. She writes with a sure command of narrative, effortlessly composing graceful sentence after graceful sentence, deftly shaping each entry, and providing historical background (about her family as well as current events), political commentary, comic anecdotes, evocative descriptions, and canny portraits of people and situations. . . . There are many light moments in Anne's account, and her situation while she was keeping the diary was far better than that of most of the Jews in Europe. (Recognizing this, in May of 1943 she wrote, "When I think about our lives here, I usually come to the conclusion that we live in a paradise compared to the Jews who aren't in hiding.")

She was also lucky to be locked up with a varied and entertaining cast of characters enduring one of history's great upheavals in a confined space where nothing could escape her gleeful detection. Anne's family was led by her father, Otto Frank, a man of such decency that four of his employees risked their lives to hide him and his family in the warehouse of the spice and fruit pectin distribution company he ran. Much beloved by Anne, who called him Pim, Otto Frank was the rock of gentle wisdom on whom the others all relied. Edith Frank, Anne's mother, worried constantly about her family's health (knowing they couldn't call a doctor if anyone fell ill), struggled to keep them well fed, and, wounded by Anne's increasing independence, vented her feelings in occasional sarcasms that further alienated her daughter. (Anne's exasperation with her mother has given rise to the book's other life as a coming-of-age how-to manual, handed to teenage girls to let them know it's normal to fight with their mothers.) The fourth Frank family member was pretty, scholarly Margot, the well-behaved older sister Anne was always being urged to emulate, but whom she privately considered too passive and accommodating. In addition to the Franks, the inhabitants of the Annex included the fussy, old-maidish dentist Alfred Dussel and the constantly quarreling van Daan family: flirtatious, hypochondriacal Mrs. van Daan, greedy, bullish Mr. van Daan, and 16-year-old Peter, quiet, sensitive, and hungry for affection (and enamored of Anne by the end of their incarceration together). Among the four non-Jews protecting them, Anne was closest to young, stylish Miep Gies, an Austrian woman married to a Dutchman, who toiled long hours keeping Otto Frank's business running (his business survived though his family did not), rode her bicycle all over Amsterdam searching for black-market provisions to feed the eight people in hiding—a near-impossible task in war-deprived Holland—and still found energy to bake cakes and bring gifts on special occasions, including a pair of high-heeled red shoes to compensate Anne for the pleasures of teen life she was missing.

THE POWER OF THE DIARY

Together, the inhabitants of the Secret Annex endured wretchedly cramped conditions (Anne had to share her tiny room with the 50-ish Dussel), airless gloom (they could never open the windows or move the curtains), scarce food supplies, and constant fear. They also shared holidays and birthdays, took correspondence courses in short-hand and foreign languages, read widely, played with the warehouse cats, followed the war by listening to the BBC at night on a secret radio, and looked forward hungrily to the daily visits of their caretakers, who brought them food, news of the outside world, and variation in the long monotony of the days.

Anne filled much of the time writing, and it's clear that the diary served as her own secret annex, a place into which she could withdraw from the irritable emotions and short tempers of the severely taxed adults scrutinizing her every move. Composing and later rewriting the diary entries enabled her to give order and meaning to the events, both frightening and trivial, taking place around her, and helped her exert some measure of control over them. At the same time, the diary gave her a way of expressing herself more freely—of being more wholly herself—than she could chance out loud. This must account in part for her cheerful equanimity as she witnessed the abrupt end to her happy childhood, although she was also graced with a remarkably sturdy ego. She was capable of great humility when she behaved badly, but unshakable in her judgments when she felt she'd been wronged (and the adults in the Annex ventilated much of their fear and frustration in petty skirmishes over the children, in which the talkative, strong-willed Anne came in for most of the abuse). She could be cranky and generous, funny and earnest, childish and unexpectedly level-headed. She saw herself clearly, and knew it. "I have one outstanding character trait that must be obvious to anyone who's known me for any length of time: I have a great deal of self-knowledge. In everything I do, I can watch myself as if I were a stranger. I can stand across from the everyday Anne and, without being biased or making excuses, watch what she's doing, both the good and the bad." This gift enabled her to present herself whole, and because she described her own behavior without vanity and that of those around her with extraordinary frankness . . . , she is the most reliable of narrators, and we trust her in everything.

As a result, the diary possesses the virtues of the best novels, with the added attribute of being true. It admits us into the inner life of its protagonist, and presents an assortment of fully realized characters, some of them heartbreakingly courageous, others admirable in their dogged attempts to preserve some semblance of normalcy under the most trying of circumstances, and others painfully, humanly weak. It has overarching suspense (the group hiding in the Annex could be betrayed at any time) as well as day-to-day suspense (will the burglar discover their hiding place; will Peter kiss Anne?). And though it doesn't have a happy ending, the ending of the story is extra-textual, explained only in the notes. The diary itself simply stops, unviolated by the worst horrors visited upon these people we have come to love. And therein lies another source of the book's power, as well as the reason it has prompted controversy in recent years.

An End That Never Comes

Anne's voice is so engaging, and possesses such a persuasive, buoyant vitality, that it seems to confirm the . . . theory that whatever happens outside the text has no meaning, and no reality. As the best novels do, Anne Frank's diary creates a world unto itself, and this world seems so real, it makes the events outside those recorded in the diary recede into shadow. Reading the book, I found my memories of innumerable film and television documentaries about the Holocaust wavering, becoming insubstantial. I had to shake my head to remind myself that those images were not fictional concoctions, but still they could not rival the vivid reality of Anne's book and Anne's world—a world that remains forever present in the text, and is reconstructed regularly in both the film made from the diary . . . and the play, which on any given night is still being performed somewhere in the world. Even in the film and the play, we never see the characters exit the Annex. The Nazis bang on the door below, and the Franks, van Daans, and Alfred Dussel cower together. Frozen in time, they wait for the end—but it is an end that never comes.

Contributing to this impression, records of what happened to the inhabitants of the Annex after they were captured are scarce. Otto Frank, the sole survivor, witnessed van Daan being led off to the gas chambers at Auschwitz in October or November 1944. Edith Frank, separated from her daughters, died alone, also at Auschwitz, in January 1945, shortly before the camp was liberated. Mrs. van Daan was shifted from Auschwitz to Buchenwald to Bergen-Belsen to Theresienstadt and perhaps to a fifth camp. She was still alive in April of 1945. After that, no one knows. "Her exact fate is unknown, although it is certain she did not survive." Peter van Daan, a healthy young man arriving at the camps late in the war, statistically had the best chance of surviving.

He was still relatively healthy when the Nazis evacuated Auschwitz, and he survived the grueling death march to Mauthausen, in Austria, only to die three days before that camp was liberated. Anne and Margot were moved from Auschwitz to Bergen-Belsen, which had the advantage of being a holding camp and not a death camp. Because they, too, began their internments late in the war and in good health, their father and friends held out great hope for their survival. But in the winter of 1945, sanitary conditions at Belsen were so miserable that typhus broke out, killing thousands of prisoners. Margot died first, leaving Anne entirely alone in the last few days of her life.

And we have no record of her thoughts during this time. Did she change her mind about the most famous line in the diaries, penned less than three weeks before she was captured—"I still believe, in spite of everything, that people are truly good at heart"? Had she been numbed by the misery she'd witnessed, or did she find the resignation she felt on April 11, 1944, after a particularly traumatic break-in to the warehouse, when she wrote, "I waited for the police and I was ready for death, like a soldier on a battlefield." Did her faith in God desert her? Did she curse humanity? In her last moments, did she murmur, "What a waste"? We don't know.

When we lose sight of her, she is pondering the duality of her own nature—the rambunctious, lively, joking personality she showed to the world, and the inner self, more thoughtful and serious, "much purer, deeper, and finer." She frets that the noisy Anne always seems to win out over the other, better, side of herself, and muses about why this is so. There is no hint of immediate danger, no sense that the end is near. Only a teenage girl working hard at forging an identity for herself.

THE DUALITY OF THE DIARIST AND OF THE DIARY

That is the view we are left with, of the girl in the process of becoming a woman. We experienced novel readers don't need the rest of the story to imagine it for ourselves, in quick, short strokes—the brilliant college career, the promising start as a journalist, the series of romances leading up to the great love affair, the long life of hard work, high spirits, and strong family affections. We can see it for her more clearly, probably, than she could ever see it for herself, and painful though it is to contemplate this life she might have had, it is far easier to look at than the life she did have—the months of fear and degradation, the loneliness and sickness, and, very possibly, the giving way of this bright, bright spirit to hopelessness. This alternative reality remains forever a blur. We don't see it; she didn't get a chance to show it to us; and we can therefore safely skirt facing the full truth of her story.

Because it omits the harshest truths of her fate, the diary has been frequently cited as a comforting document—see, even in the midst of history's worst depredations, the human spirit is not quelled, goodness and beauty endure. And this is also the source of the controversy around the book—that it has been used to blunt the reality of the Holocaust as much as it has been used to vivify it; that people take comfort in Anne's faith in humanity rather than face the brutal reality that she was destroyed. In our celebrity-infatuated, fame-worshipping times, the thought may also sneak in that perhaps it's okay, maybe it was worth it, because she wrote a great book and she got her wish and became world famous, and her book survives even if she did not. But, as Primo Levi responded whenever asked if maybe he was sent to Auschwitz because he was "meant" to survive to write the great books he wrote about his experiences, no book is worth this degree of human suffering. No God could orchestrate such unspeakable events in order to produce a mere book. Miep Gies said the same thing a little differently.... "Always, every day of my life, I've wished that things had been different. That even had Anne's diary been lost to the world, Anne and the others might somehow have been saved. Not a day goes by that I do not grieve for them."

Anne Frank's *Diary* Is More Poignant Because It Ignores the Horror of the Holocaust

Ann Birstein and Alfred Kazin

Anne Frank did not limit her writings to a diary. She wrote short stories, fables, personal reminiscences, and essays as well, all of which were included in a book of her works published in the 1950s. In the following excerpt from the Introduction to that book, Ann Birstein and Alfred Kazin assert their view of Anne Frank and of her *Diary*—the sensibility expressed in the telling and interpretation of ordinary events and the evidence of compassion for human suffering. That Anne Frank's *Diary* does not deal with horror directly does not mean that it—or Anne —was escapist in nature. The *Diary* moves readers, conclude Birstein and Kazin, precisely because it is not the usual gory literature of war and because "its author has the strength to see, to hope, to remember."

In March 1945, a young girl died in Bergen-Belsen, unaware that she was leaving behind her a work that shed the first tiny human light on an episode in history that was unspeakably inhuman. She was a lovely girl, not quite sixteen when she died, with enormous dark gray eyes, a pretty little mouth, and a very brave heart. But like any awkward and self-conscious adolescent, she was weighed down by a sense of her shortcomings. She worried about her looks; she thought of herself as a coward, so often full of fear that she never realized how heroically she overcame it. Certainly, it would have been beyond her to imagine that the diary she kept for two years would have an impact on the entire world; how could it when the events of her lifetime were so enor-

From the Introduction by Alfred Kazin and Ann Birstein to *The Works of Anne Frank* by Anne Frank, copyright ©1959 by Otto H. Frank. Used by permission of Doubleday, a division of Bantam Doubleday Dell Publishing Group, Inc.

mous she could only seem puny by comparison? Her only real certainty was that she meant to be a writer anyway, and that her subject would have to be the world in which she found herself alive, no matter how terrible or even how unaccountably lovely her experiences in it might seem. For two years before her arrest she wrote all the time. She wrote while she was in hiding from the Nazis and could not take one step outdoors or in the daytime speak above a whisper. She wrote although the bombs came down so heavily at night that she fled for comfort into her father's bed. She wrote so steadily that by the time she was fifteen she had finished the equivalent of two books, one the *Diary,* the other a collection of short stories, essays, and reminiscences. As she said, with amazement at her own daring, she wrote because, "I want to go on living even after my death!" She has—reminding us that each of those millions who died in agony and despair, each of those victims whom the Nazis "exterminated" was, like Anne Frank, a separate and precious human spirit. . . .

A Sense of Posterity

On a hot July morning in 1942 [the Franks] went into hiding, walking across Amsterdam in the pouring rain to a small group of rooms behind Mr. Frank's former offices. Here they and four others were to stay cooped up for more than two years, until the Dutch Green Police routed them out on August 4, 1944; and here Anne's diary . . . was to grow and grow until, like all truly remarkable books, it finally outgrew its own author.

In a certain sense, however, it isn't fair to call *The Diary of a Young Girl* a diary at all, since from the very first it was more to her than a purely personal record of triumphs and defeats. Always she had toward her own experience the marvelous ambivalence of the born novelist, and immediately after claiming that "neither I—nor for that matter anyone else—will be interested in the unbosomings of a thirteen-year-old schoolgirl" on the very same page of her journal she has already chosen a literary form—the entries will be in the shape of letters to an imaginary girl named Kitty—and embarked on a concise sketch, not only of her own life, but of general conditions in Holland. This same uncanny sense of an unseen audience, actually of posterity, prevails throughout her work. Scared out of her wits as she must have been when she went into hiding, one of the first things she writes about it is a detailed description of the hiding place and the bits and pieces of furnishings that went into it. When new people arrive ... she has them down on paper practically the minute they are through the door. With a writer's eye for how much is implied in the ordinary events of an ordinary day, she describes a typical morning, afternoon, and evening in the annexe; how they went to the toilet; where they slept; what they talked about while they peeled potatoes and shelled peas and stuffed sausages....

To everything that happened to her, to everything that she felt, Anne gave a kind of permanence by transcribing it, and day after day she went on adding still another segment to the world she was creating.... In her diary, where her subject chose her, its vividness and poignance are overwhelming. We can see them all....

What makes her achievement really amazing is how little, aside from her own natural gifts of observation and her sense of humor, she had to work with. Other people have countrysides and multitudes. For Anne, the one boy upstairs was love; a single chestnut tree seen from her window, nature; a patch of blue sky—heaven. No wonder that soon she began to think of her diary and some of her sketches as the basis for a book after the war. *Het Achterhuis* (The House Behind) she meant to call it—a perfect title for the first book of a young girl, suggesting mystery and suspense and excitement; she even had a list of pseudonyms for the people in it, pseudonyms which are used in this present edition.

A SENSE OF HUMANITY

But the duality of Anne's nature, that quality of mind that made her turn to her writing for solace and relief, that made of her diary her "only friend" and the first thing she packed when she went into hiding, was exactly what would not let her rest. Like all young growing things, Anne, forced into a premature ripeness by the terrible intensity of events, yearned and struggled for the light. It was not enough to take her own little part in the day's happenings, to chatter and laugh and cry with everyone else; the spectator in her kept pressing her to ask the meaning of it all, kept goading her into a search that could only take her deeper and deeper into the most painful realms of solitude. We tend to think of Anne now as pure innocence in captivity. But her mind and heart were never held captive by herself or anyone, and as for her innocence—it was the last thing she ever thought about. On the contrary, she wanted to take it all on her own shoulders, she considered herself responsible for everything, not only her own destiny—if she was permitted to live it out—but also the fate of everyone else who suffered. ". . . I believe," she said, "that God wants to try me . . . I'm restless, I go from one room to the other, breathe through the crack of a closed window, feel my heart beating, as if it is saying, 'Can't you satisfy my longings at last?'. . . I believe that it's spring within me, I feel that spring is awakening. I feel it in my whole body and soul." But still she kept at it, crying herself out when she could, and then trying to unloose her own pity for herself into a great stream of compassion for all suffering humanity. How could she feel sorry for herself when just outside her door children were running about half naked, begging food from passers-by, and people did not dare leave their homes for fear that when they came back no one would be left in them? It was not enough to be glad of her own precarious safety; one had to ask why even this was denied others. . . . And what about all Jews? What purpose was there in their common agony? "Who has inflicted this upon us? What has made us different from other people? Who has allowed us to suffer so terribly until now?"

Child or not, anyone who asks such questions can never find an answer, only the strength of spirit to go on searching. Anne found her strength in her love of the very world which was denied her. Often in their "Secret Annexe" they talked of the best cure for unhappiness, and Mrs. Frank's advice was to remember those who were even more unhappy. But to Anne, though no one listened to her, this could add only more misery to a cup already overflowing with it. "I simply can't build up my hopes on a foundation consisting of confusion, misery, and death. I see the world gradually being turned into a wilderness, I hear the ever approaching thunder, which will destroy us too, I can feel the sufferings of millions and yet, if I look up into the heavens, I think that this cruelty too will end, and that peace and tranquillity will return again." What she saw when she looked up was a reminder that despite all the ugliness inflicted on it, the world was still incredibly beautiful, and each time she could not get over the miracle of it. . . .

Perhaps when she went to bed on the night of August 3,

1944, her last thought was of her own blessedness: her youth, her strength, her love for all the people and the growing things around her, her closeness to God, who had provided them. There is no way of knowing. On the next morning, the Dutch Nazi police suddenly stormed through the concealed doorway of the annexe with drawn revolvers and took all its inhabitants away. In a heap of papers and books which the police had dumped on the floor during their search for money and valuables, Miep and Elli later found the notebooks Anne had kept so carefully. They put them aside for the day when Anne would come back for them, a time which never came. . . .

THE MAKING OF A LEGEND

Only the father returned—to learn that he alone was left and to be given his daughter's notebooks by Miep and Elli. The little books must have seemed pathetic enough to Otto Frank when, after his own slow recovery to health, he returned to Amsterdam to learn, after agonizing inquiries, that his wife and two children were dead. The diary was peculiarly heartbreaking, not only in its reminder of all that eight people had lived through and hoped for in more than two years of captivity, but in its revelation of Anne. Lies Goosens remembers Otto Frank's saying to her, when the *Diary* was first published: "Anne developed under our eyes in that room, but we went on treating her as though she still was a giddy little girl. All of us were too wrapped up in our own troubles to give her the understanding that she needed.". . .

Anne Frank has become a universal legend. Out of the millions who were gassed, burned, shot, hanged, starved, tortured, buried alive, the young girl who died so "peacefully" in Bergen-Belsen, almost in unconscious sympathy with her dead sister Margot, has become a prime symbol of the innocence of all those who died in the middle of the twentieth century at the hands of the most powerful state in western Europe. Perhaps more than any of the known dead, and certainly more than the now nameless ones who died scratching the ceilings of the gas chambers in the last agonized struggle against death, the girl born in Frankfurt of an upper-class Jewish family, whose father was a German officer in World War I, has become the personal example of the heartlessness, the bestiality, the still unbelievable cruelty of Germans in World War II. Upon her, at least, all agree; in her all peoples, in the uneasy peace since 1945 that is no peace, can find a moment's occasion for compassion and awareness. When *The Diary of Anne Frank* was produced on the Dutch stage, royalty wept; and by now, as everyone knows, Germans who had wept for no one but themselves, who had not allowed themselves to recognize the horror in their midst . . . have wept in theaters over Anne Frank. In October

---

THROUGH A POWERFUL MAGNIFYING GLASS

Anne Frank had the ability to look inside herself and explain what she saw and how she felt. On Tuesday, March 7, 1944, she wrote in her diary about the changes that had taken place in her since 1942.

I look upon my life up till the New Year, as it were, through a powerful magnifying glass. The sunny life at home, then coming here in 1942, the sudden change, the quarrels, the bickerings. I couldn't understand it, I was taken by surprise, and the only way I could keep up some bearing was by being impertinent.

The first half of 1943: my fits of crying, the loneliness, how I slowly began to see all my faults and shortcomings, which are so great and which seemed much greater then. During the day I deliberately talked about anything and everything that was farthest from my thoughts, tried to draw Pim to me; but couldn't. Alone I had to face the difficult task of changing myself, to stop the everlasting reproaches, which were so oppressive and which reduced me to such terrible despondency.

Things improved slightly in the second half of the year, I became a young woman and was treated more like a grownup. I started to think, and write stories, and came to the conclusion that the others no longer had the right to throw me about like an india-rubber ball. I wanted to change in accordance with my own desires. But *one* thing that struck me even more was when I realized that even Daddy would never become my confidant over everything. I didn't want to trust anyone but myself any more.

At the beginning of the New Year: the second great change, my dream. . . . And with it I discovered my longing, not for a girl friend, but for a boy friend. I also discovered my inward happiness and my defensive armor of superficiality and gaiety. In due time I quieted down and discovered my boundless desire for all that is beautiful and good.

And in the evening, when I lie in bed and end my prayers with the words, "I thank you, God, for all that is good and dear and beautiful," I am filled with joy.

1956, when the play opened in seven German cities to silent audiences, there was by all accounts unexpected horror and dismay. Alfred Werner, in a study of "Germany's New Flagellants" (*The American Scholar,* Spring 1958), reports that not until 1956 was there a mass emotion of expiation in Germany, and that it started with the Hacketts' play. The play "broke through the tough shell that the German had grown around his soul.". . .

The production of *Das Tagebuch der Anne Frank* coincided with what in certain intellectual circles became a pro-Jewish philosophy, a return to the abstraction of the "noble Jew" among the German intellectuals of the Enlightenment. It is for this reason that Anne Frank has symbolized so much—so peculiarly much—in current German thought. A sixteen-year-old girl, participant in [a 1957] Belsen pilgrimage, wrote a letter published in newspapers all over the Bonn Republic: "I have sworn that we must do better! All must be made to realize that the highest and the most beautiful being is man—regardless of whether he is a Jew, a Dane, a Russian, an Englishman, a Frenchman, or a German. . . .

"Anne, you did not die in vain. We, today's youth, want to believe in what is good in man—as you did. . . . We shall never forget you and all those innocent people who had to die like you. We do not want to forget, and we must never forget.". . .

THE ACCEPTANCE OF INNOCENCE

The figure of universally accepted innocence, a young girl, is so perfect a subject that young people can identify with her; older people can pity her; the world can almost believe that it has made peace with itself over the unknown grave of Anne Frank. . . . *The Diary Of Anne Frank* does not deal with horror—at least not directly; yet this, though it makes it too easy for all of us not to think of the horror at all, is also what makes both book and play *possible.* It was not only Germans who laughed derisively when shown the first films of the concentration camps; so did the English in Piccadilly newsreel theaters. The fact is that certain events in our time, prime and unforgettable images of human suffering and degradation, seem incredible to us even when we remember them, and are ungraspable even when we face them.

Anne Frank herself felt this about many horrors in her young life. . . . The day the Frank family was taken off to the German detention camp was a beautiful summer day.

Anne's father told Ernst Schnabel, "As we rode toward Westerbork . . . Anne would not move from the window. Outside,
it was summer. Meadows, stubble fields, and villages flew
by. The telephone wires along the right of way curvetted up
and down along the windows. It was like freedom." It must
have seemed incredible to look at beautiful summer days,
the peaceful summer scene, when she was in hiding because she was a Jew, or when she was in a train being led
off to a concentration camp. It is this radical injustice, this
unaccountability, that characterizes for children their most
painful experiences; the anthropomorphic child in all of us
can still feel the injustice of slipping out of life while someone else is yawning, or drinking beer. In the world of totali-
tarianism, the victim suffers from the illogic of his fate as
well as the terror of death. . . . It was "absurd" as well as unspeakable to put children into concentration camps; "absurd" as well as unforgivable to allow millions upon millions of innocent civilians, Jews and non-Jews, to die as they
did. But absurd, out of focus, beyond the human scale, utterly illogical and often ungraspable as the death of an innocent fifteen-year-old girl at the hands of the Third Reich
may be, it is a fact. It is a fact that never can be forgotten, that
never will be forgotten. But it is also a fact that the reality of
what certain people have had to endure in our time can be
grasped humanly and politically only because of the modu-
lation of a document like *The Diary of a Young Girl,* which
permits us to see certain experiences in a frame, in a thoroughly human setting, so that we can bear them at all.

THE SURVIVAL OF HOPE

Anne Frank's *Diary* has rarely been subjected to criticism.
The dramatic economy of the book has moved its readers
just as much as the fate of its author has served as an occasion of emotion. Yet it has been suggested that Anne was unable to confront the hideousness of her experience, that her
diary was an escape into the ideal. And in one sense this
"evasion" of reality, if one may so call it, though improbable
coming from people who have never had to face anything
like Anne Frank's experience, is perfectly true. It may be that
the "ideal" quality of the book accounts for the universal acceptance of the *Diary;* has made it possible for Germans to
ease their souls sitting in a theater; for Jews to honor their
dead; for the Dutch and the French to remember their suf-

fering under the occupation; for adolescent children to take imaginative refuge from their problems. And yet it is a fact that Anne Frank's wholly domestic picture of life works toward the understanding of her true situation, rather than the other way around. For truthfully direct "war literature," naked shots of the ultimate horror, are hard for everyone to get down. . . . In the "ideal" world of Anne Frank's diary, in the preoccupation with potato peels, a young girl's discovery of puberty, there is the truth of life as human curiosity and sensitivity and fellowship—while outside, the green and gray German army lorries trundle past bearing their helpless Jewish victims to the slaughter heap.

The Diary of a Young Girl has survived its author and most of her family, as it has already survived so many books about the war, because the faithfulness with which it records an unusual experience reminds us—as opposition to Nazism on its own terms never can—of the sweetness and goodness that are possible in a world where a few souls still have good will. The *Diary* moves us because its author had the strength to see, to remember, to hope. . . .

Anne Frank died of typhus in the hell of Bergen-Belsen. Yet when one weeps for her it is not out of pity. Pity is for the faceless and the weak. Events could only make Anne helpless. And though it is a miracle that her diary and her little stories and essays have survived at all, the real miracle is that in the young girl who wrote them life was so strong to begin with.

Anne Frank:
A Tale of Morality

Henry F. Pommer

In an article written for *Judaism* magazine in 1960, Henry F. Pommer speaks about the legend that has enveloped Anne Frank and about her abilities and development as a writer. In the following excerpt from that article, Pommer maintains that Frank's fame rests as much on the knowledge of her life as of her death. Anne Frank's diary, which is a mixture of good and bad writing, is an adolescent record of history that formed the foundation of the legend and Frank's importance as a historical figure. Some critics contend that the truths of Anne's *Diary* are not about one group or culture but about humanity. Others view the *Diary* primarily as an intimate and frank account of adolescence written by a young girl with an exceptional ability for self-analysis.

The quality of both her death and her life have given Anne Frank an extraordinary status in our culture. Antigone represents a willingness to die for principles; Juliet's is the tragedy of ironic confusion; Marguerite was the victim of her own and Faust's sensuality; St. Joan was martyred by jealous institutions. Anne was destroyed by a pattern of evil perhaps not unique to our century, but at least unique within Western culture of the past two thousand years.

But her fame rests on knowledge of her life as much as of her death. She is not a fictional character like Juliet or Tolstoy's Natasha, nor a girl with widespread and immediate effects like St. Joan or the young Cleopatra. Yet she shares with Cleopatra and St. Joan the fact of being historical; and her life is already, like theirs, the source of a legend. As an historical figure relatively unimportant to her immediate contemporaries but affecting a larger and larger circle after her

Reprinted by permission fom Henry F. Pommer, "The Legend and Art of Anne Frank," *JUDAISM*, vol. 9, no. 1, Winter 1960, pp. 37–46. Copyright 1960, American Jewish Congress.

death, she is most like St. Thérèse of Lisieux. But over all these girls from Antigone to St. Thérèse, Anne has the great advantage that she left a diary. Therefore, we need not know her through the documents of her contemporaries or the professional imagination of middle-aged authors. Her legend lacks the support of patriotic and ecclesiastical power, but it has the strength of her authentic, self-drawn portrait.

A FOCUS ON HUMANITY

Some writers have considered the diary as primarily "one of the most moving stories that anyone, anywhere, has managed to tell about World War II." At Oradour-sur-Glane, where Nazis wantonly destroyed the entire population, is printed "Remember," and in the ruins of bomb-destroyed Coventry has been carved "Father Forgive." Anne's diary helps us remember what there is to forgive.

[The] truths of Anne's history, the bitter as well as the sweet, are not about Germans alone or Dutchmen or Jews, but humanity. And these truths must be recalled whenever we try to measure human nature, to estimate its heights and depths, its capacities for good and evil. The extremes of cruelty temper all our hopes. On the other hand, a young person is supposed to have once asked Justice Felix Frankfurter "And how do you know that the human race is *worth* saving?" The Justice replied, "I have read Anne Frank's diary."

ADOLESCENCE AND SELF-ANALYSIS

A second group of critics has praised the diary as primarily an intimate account of adolescence. For these it is of only secondary importance that Anne hid with her family in an attic of old Amsterdam; of primary importance is her frankness in telling what it is like to grow up.

Often she was difficult to live with. Tensions were almost inevitable for eight people living with so many restrictions in such cramped quarters, but Anne seems to have done more than her share to stir up ill will. She had a temper, and was not always either anxious or able to control it. At times she must have been obnoxiously precocious in telling the other hiders what they were like; she may have appeared very patronizing at times; particularly in dealing with Margot about Peter. She was very critical of her mother, very fond of her father, and from time to time hurt both of them deeply. Her sense of justice, her loathing of whatever was

pompous or artificial, and her desire to be treated as an
adult led to frequent quarrels with Mr. and Mrs. Van Daan,
and with Mr. Dussel.

Bit by bit, however, these evidences of immaturity and of
being difficult decrease. Mixed with them, yet gradually re-
placing them, came the actions and reactions of a more mature young woman.

Any diary of a young girl who hid in Amsterdam during
the Nazi occupation, who described her first protracted love
affair, and who was a person of breeding, humor, religious
sensitivity, and courage might well interest us. But Anne had
one further trait of the utmost importance for her own maturity and for what she wrote: an unusual ability for self-
analysis. She knew she had moods, and she could write elo-
quently about them—about loneliness, for example. But she
could also step outside her moods in order to evaluate them
and herself in them.

One of the clearest evidences of objectivity was her ability to see a moral ambiguity in her enjoying relative security
while other Jews suffered worse fates:

> I saw two Jews through the curtain yesterday. I could hardly
> believe my eyes; it was a horrible feeling, just as if I'd be-
> trayed them and was now watching them in their misery.

This is the honesty concerning oneself out of which are
born humor, maturity, and one kind of ability to write well.

AN ABILITY AS A WRITER

Anne could write well. Her self-consciousness and skill as
an author receive only implicit acknowledgement if we regard her diary as no more than an educative historical document or an intimate disclosure of adolescence. W.A. Dar-
lington is probably correct in predicting that

> in time to come, when the horrors of Nazi occupation in Eu-
> rope are no longer quite so fresh in quite so many minds and
> "The Diary of Anne Frank" comes to be judged purely on its
> merits as a play, the piece will . . . lose its place on the stage.

But Anne's diary may have a longer life. It is, to be sure, a
mixture of good and bad writing—but so, too, are the diaries
of Pepys, Samuel Sewall, and William Byrd.

Some people have combed the external record of Anne's
life for evidence of her ability as a writer.

It was to be expected that little external evidence of Anne's
talent would be found. When she went into hiding, she was

not a diarist worthy of much attention. During the twenty-five months in the Secret Annexe, the world of her thought was a secret within a secret—a secret so well kept that even her father confessed, when the diary was first published, "I never realized my little Anna was so deep." After she had left the Annexe, the brutality of guards, shortages of food, epidemics of disease, separation from loved ones, and the prospect of gas chambers must have left Anne little time to think about writing, and certainly gave her companions little interest in what her literary talents might be. Ever so much more important was whether she could beg a piece of zwieback.

When we turn to the diary itself, we find that if her affair with Peter is the most striking measure of her change towards maturity, the second most striking is the clarification of her desire to be a writer. The third entry begins the development.

> I haven't written for a few days, because I wanted first of all to think about my diary. It's an odd idea for someone like me to keep a diary; not only because I have never done so before, but because it seems to me that neither I—nor for that matter anyone else—will be interested in the unbosomings of a thirteen-year-old schoolgirl. Still, what does that matter? I want to write, but more than that, I want to bring out all kinds of things that lie buried deep in my heart....

> There is no doubt that paper is patient and as I don't intend to show this ... "diary," to anyone, unless I find a real friend, boy or girl, probably nobody cares. And now I come to the root of the matter, the reason for my starting a diary: it is that I have no such real friend....

> It's the same with all my friends, just fun and joking, nothing more. I can never bring myself to talk of anything outside the common round....

> Hence, this diary. In order to enhance in my mind's eye the picture of the friend for whom I have waited so long, I don't want to set down a series of bald facts in a diary like most people do, but I want this diary itself to be my friend, and I shall call my friend Kitty.

After this early entry the diary shows a progressively self-conscious artistry reflected in the beginnings of certain letters to Kitty such as

> Now that we have been in the "Secret Annexe" for over a year, you know something of our lives, but some of it is quite indescribable.... To give you a closer look ..., now and again I intend to give you a description of an ordinary day. Today I'm beginning with the evening and the night.... (August 4, 1943).

> I asked myself this morning whether you don't sometimes feel rather like a cow who has had to chew over all the old pieces of news again and again, and who finally yawns loudly and silently wishes that Anne would occasionally find something new.... (January 28, 1944).

> Perhaps it would be entertaining for you—though not in the least for me—to hear what we are going to eat today.... (March 14,1944).

AN ADOLESCENT RECORD OF HISTORY

That her diary might itself be the basis of a published work may not have occurred to Anne before March 29, 1944, when

> Bolkestein, an M.P., was speaking on the Dutch News from London, and ... said that they ought to make a collection of diaries and letters after the war. Of course, they all made a rush at my diary immediately. Just imagine how interesting it would be if I were to publish a romance of the "Secret Annexe." The title alone would be enough to make people think it was a detective story.

> But, seriously, it would seem quite funny ten years after the war if we Jews were to tell how we lived and what we ate and talked about here.

After the entry of March 29, Anne's expressed desires to be a journalist, and then a famous writer, grew more numerous. Writing would, she hoped, enable her to live after her death; she wrote short stories, even wanting to submit them for publication.

The chief literary merit of the diary is its permitting us to know intimately Anne's young, eager, difficult, lovable self. We follow the quick alternations of her great gaiety and sometimes equally great depression, and we benefit from the introspections generated by her sharply contrasting moods. Some pages read as though they had been written in the security of a Long Island suburbia; on the next page we are plunged into Nazi terror; and both passages use vivid details. Sometimes our delight is simply in her charm, as in "Daddy always says I'm prudish and vain but that's not true. I'm just simply vain." At other times her wisdom surprises us, as in her distinction that "laziness may *appear* attractive, but work *gives* satisfaction." She sensed the need for variety in reporting, and used effective techniques for achieving it. Life in the Secret Annexe was terribly repetitious, but there is little repetition in the diary itself.

Even if the last entry told of Jews liberated by the arrival of Allied armies in Amsterdam, the book would still have real interest and value. And it would still have its chief moral significance. Both diary and play illustrate D.H. Lawrence's contention that

> the essential function of art is moral. Not aesthetic, nor decorative, not pastime and recreation. But moral.... But a passionate, implicit morality, not didactic. A morality which changes the blood, rather than the mind. Changes the blood first. The mind follows later in the wake.

Because of Anne Frank's art, this change in blood and then in mind sometimes takes the direction of brotherhood. At those moments her legend receives fresh life, and her adolescent record of history helps to make history less adolescent.

The Popularity of Anne Frank's *Diary* Denies the Real Lesson of the Holocaust

Bruno Bettelheim

Austrian-born Bruno Bettelheim survived the concentration camps of Dachau and Buchenwald and immigrated to the United States in 1939. A prominent child psychologist and psychoanalyst, he was a professor of education, psychology, and psychiatry at the University of Chicago and an award-winning author. In this controversial essay, using Anne Frank and her family as an example, Bettelheim purports to explain why millions of people went to their deaths with little or no resistance during the Nazi persecution of the Jews. The great popularity of the *Diary,* argues Bettelheim, can be attributed to the tendency of most people to deny the reality of the concentration camps.

When the world first learned about the concentration camps, most civilized people felt the horrors committed in them to be uncanny. It came as a shock to their pride that supposedly civilized nations could stoop to such inhuman acts. The implication that modern man has such inadequate control over his cruelty was felt as a threat. Three different psychological mechanisms were most frequently used for dealing with the phenomenon of the concentration camp:

(a) its applicability to man in general was denied by asserting—contrary to available evidence—that the acts of torture were committed by a small group of insane or perverted persons;

(b) the truth of the reports was denied by ascribing them to deliberate propaganda (this method was favored by the

German government, which called all reports on terror in the camps horror propaganda—*Greuelpropaganda*);

(c) the reports were believed, but the knowledge of the terror was repressed as soon as possible.

All three mechanisms could be seen at work after liberation. . . .

The universal success of *The Diary of Anne Frank* suggests how much of the tendency to deny the reality of the camps is still with us, while her story itself demonstrates how such denial can hasten our own destruction. (I cannot comment, I should point out, on what actually happened to the Frank family—only on the account given in Anne's *Diary* and in the play and movie based on it.) It is an onerous task to take apart so humane and moving a story, which has aroused so much compassion for gentle Anne Frank. But I believe that its world-wide acclaim cannot be explained unless we recognize our wish to forget the gas chambers and to glorify the ability to retreat into an extremely private world, clinging to the usual daily attitudes even in a holocaust.

THE FRANK FAMILY'S FATAL ATTITUDE

The Frank family's attitude that life could be carried on as usual was glorified precisely because it did lead to their destruction. By glorifying it in this way, we were able to ignore the crucial lesson of the story—that such an attitude can be fatal in extreme social circumstances.

While the Franks were making their preparations for going passively into hiding, thousands of other Jews in Holland and elsewhere in Europe were trying to escape to the Free World, in order to survive or to be able to fight. Others who could not do so went underground—not simply to hide from the SS and wait for the day when they would be caught—but to fight against Germans and for humanity. We gather from the *Diary*, however, that the chief desire of the Frank family was to go on with life as nearly as possible in the usual fashion.

Little Anne, too, wanted only to go on with life as usual, and nobody can blame her. But hers was certainly not a necessary fate, much less a heroic one; it was a senseless fate. The Franks could have faced the facts as did many Jews living in Holland. Anne could have had a good chance to survive, as did many Jewish children in Holland. But for that she would have had to be separated from her parents and gone to live with a Dutch family as their own child.

Everybody who recognized the obvious knew that the hardest way to go underground was to do it as a family; to hide as a family made detection by the SS most likely. The Franks, with their excellent connections among gentile Dutch families, might well have been able to hide out singly, each with a different family. But instead it would seem that the main principle of their planning was to continue as much as possible with the kind of family life they were accustomed to. Any other course would have meant not merely giving up their beloved family life, but also accepting the reality of man's inhumanity to man. Most of all it would have forced them to accept that going on with life as usual was not an absolute value, but can sometimes be the most destructive of all attitudes.

There is little doubt that the Franks, who were able to provide themselves with so much, could have provided themselves with a gun or two had they wished. They could have shot down at least one or two of the "green police" who came for them. There was no surplus of such police. The loss of an SS with every Jew arrested would have noticeably hindered the functioning of the police state. The fate of the Franks wouldn't have been very different, because they all died anyway except for Anne's father. But they could have sold their lives dearly instead of walking to their death.

There is good reason why the enormously successful play ends with Anne stating her belief in the good in all men. What is evaded is the importance of accepting the gas chambers as real so that never again will they be allowed to exist. If all men are basically good—if going on with intimate family living, no matter what else, is what is to be most admired—then indeed we can all go on with life as usual and forget about Auschwitz. Except that Anne Frank died because her parents could not get themselves to believe in Auschwitz. And her story found wide acclaim because for us too, it denies implicitly that Auschwitz ever existed. If all men are good, there was never an Auschwitz.

AN INNER DISINTEGRATION

This failure of the Frank family only reflects the failure of a great many others when faced with the threat of the total Nazi state. It is a failure, I suggest, which deserves close examination and can reveal valuable lessons for us today.

In my studies of the Nazi system I have pointed out that the submission of the persecuted to the total power of the state often led both to the disintegration of what had once seemed well-integrated personalities and to a return to infantile attitudes. . . .

Many [concentration camp prisoners] persuaded themselves that they, out of all the others, would be spared. Many more simply disbelieved in the possibility of their own death. Not believing in it, they did not prepare for it; they made no plans for defending their lives if and when death would become inescapable. It is true that defending their lives before such a time might have hastened their death, and so, up to a point, they were protecting themselves by "rolling with the punches" of the enemy. But beyond that point it was destructive of both one's own life and that of others who might have survived if one had risked one's own life. The longer one "rolls" with the punches, the more likely it becomes that one will no longer have the strength to resist when death becomes imminent. This is particularly true if yielding to the enemy is accompanied not by an inner strengthening of the personality—but by an inner disintegration. (We can observe such a disintegration among the Franks, who bickered with each other over trifles, instead of supporting each other's desire to resist the demoralizing impact of their living conditions.)

Those who did not deny validity to death, who neither denied nor repressed its possibility—who embraced no childish belief in their indestructibility—were those who prepared for it in time as a real possibility. It meant risking one's life for a self-chosen purpose and in doing so, saving one's own life or that of others, or both. When Jews in Germany were restricted to their homes, those who did not succumb to inertia took the new restrictions as a warning that it was high time to go underground, join the Resistance movement, provide themselves with forged papers, and so on, if they had not done so long ago. Most of them survived.

Some distant relatives of mine may furnish an example. Early in the war, a young man living in a small Hungarian town banded together with a number of other Jews to prepare against a German invasion. As soon as the Nazis imposed curfews on the Jews, his group left for Budapest—the bigger the city, the better the chances for escaping detection. There, similar groups from other towns converged and joined those of Budapest. From among them they selected typically "Aryan"-looking men, who equipped themselves with false papers and immediately joined the Hungarian SS. They were then able to warn of impending persecution, to report in advance when a particular district would be searched, etc.

This worked so well that most of the groups survived intact. But they had also equipped themselves with small arms, so that when detected they could put up enough of a fight for the majority to escape while a few would die fighting to gain time for the escape. . . .

(Compare these arrangements to the Franks' selection of a hiding place that was basically a trap without an outlet: In all their months there, no emergency escape route was constructed through which some of their group could at least have tried to escape while one or two of the men blocked and defended one of the small entrances with a homemade barricade. Compare also, Mr. Frank's teaching typically academic high-school subjects to the youngsters, rather than how to make a getaway: a token of the same inability to face the possibility of death.)

POSSESSIONS: A REASON TO DIE

My young relative was unable to convince some members of his family to go with him when he left. . . . He could not convince them to move out of their homes, to leave their possessions. . . .

When I was a prisoner in Buchenwald, I talked to hundreds of German Jewish prisoners who were brought there in the fall of 1938. I asked them why they had not left Germany because of the utterly degrading conditions they were subjected to. Their answer was: How could we leave? It would have meant giving up our homes, our places of business. Their earthly belongings had so taken possession of them that they could not move; instead of using them, they were dominated by them. (The Franks, too, postponed going into hiding because they wished first to transfer more of their possessions to their hideout. They postponed it so long that it was nearly too late for Anne's sister, who was called to the SS.)

How the investing of personal property with one's life energy could make people die bit by bit was demonstrated throughout the Nazi persecution of the Jews. At the time of the first boycott of Jewish stores the chief external goal of the Nazis was the possessions of the Jews. They even let Jews take some of them out of the country if they would just go, leaving the bulk of their property behind. For a long time the intention of the Nazis, and of their first discriminatory laws, was to force undesirable minorities, including Jews, into emigration. Only when this did not work was the extermination policy instituted, though it also followed the inner logic of the Nazi racial ideology. . . .

Many Jews in Poland who did not believe in life-as-usual survived the second world war. As the Germans approached, they left everything behind and fled to Russia, much as many of them distrusted the Soviet system. But there, while perhaps citizens of a second order, they were at least accepted as human beings. Those who stayed on to continue life-as-usual moved toward their own destruction and perished. Thus in the deepest sense the walk to the gas chamber was only the last consequence of a philosophy of life-as-usual. It was the final step of surrender to the death instinct, which might also be called the principle of inertia. The first step was taken long before arrival at the death camp.

CHAPTER 3

The Legacy of *The Diary of a Young Girl*

Searching for the Real Anne Frank

Ernst Schnabel

In the late 1950s, novelist, dramatist, and short-story writer Ernst Schnabel set out to discover what made Anne Frank's diary so powerful. Did the strength of the diary emanate from the story it told? Or was the strength in the storyteller herself? What was the real Anne like? Was she really the same person as the legendary Anne? Schnabel tracked down and interviewed more than forty people who had known Anne Frank or whose paths had crossed hers at one time or another during her short lifetime. The interviews formed the basis of his book *Anne Frank: A Portrait in Courage.* The following excerpt from the book focuses on Schnabel's interview with Madame van der Waal, the mother of one of Anne's best friends.

It was late evening before I found my way out to Amsterdam-West, where Jopie van der Waal now lives. . . . Jopie was Anne's best friend. . . .

I was out of luck and did not find Jopie at home. She had gone out with her husband, leaving her baby rosily asleep in its crib, while her mother sat guard over its slumber. But Madame van der Waal quickly observed that perhaps it was not such bad luck after all, since mothers have a better memory than children. . . .

ANNE: A GREAT PERSONALITY

Madame van der Waal, French by birth, married a Hollander and has been living in Amsterdam since she was quite young. But to this day she cannot really manage Dutch. It gratified her to hear that I could not really manage it either, and she simply ignored my objection that my French was scarcely better.

From Ernst Schnabel, *Anne Frank: A Portrait in Courage,* translated from the German by Richard and Clara Winston (New York: Harcourt, Brace & World). Copyright © Fischer Bücherei KG, Frankfurt am Main, 1958. All rights with Fischer Taschenbuch Verlag GmbH, Frankfurt am Main.

"Anne?" she said. "Aaah, Anne was a little monkey. *Très intelligent, très feminine.*... And just thirteen, consider that!" Madame exclaimed, clapping her hands over her breast. "She was a great personality. A human soul. *Une femme*! Why, recently I went to Bijenkorf—that is the big department store on the Damrak—and all of a sudden I saw Anne's picture right in front of me. Not in the book department, not a bit of it. It stood on an ordinary shelf, with a few flowers alongside it, and in front of it the salesgirl sold me thread.... No, I tell you," Madame said, shaking her finger as if she were protesting against the invisible Dark Angel in the air, "we have not lost her."

There was no need for me to put questions to Madame. What she had to say came tumbling out of her.

Jopie had seen the play [based on Anne Frank's life], on opening night. She had sat near the Queen, and she had reported that the Queen's face had been deeply flushed from excitement and emotion. "And now, I ask you, Anne was only a child, after all. Remember that, a child!

"I myself," Madame continued, "have only read her diary, but when I read it Anne appeared before me. I saw her, alive. But she had not come to me, no, it was not like that. She drew me to her, to herself, into her strange, grotesque world which none of us knew a thing about."

A MESSAGE STRAIGHT FROM THE HEART

"No—" suddenly Madame's voice became strong and positive—"she is not lost to us. Jopie admits I'm right. There's Jopie's baby sleeping over there. Have you seen it? To think that here we already have the next generation."

Madame delighted me. She was in her sixties, with gray hair which at the moment was somewhat disarrayed; her eyes flashed as she talked with me. Her embroidery lay untouched in her lap. There was something sweet, knowing, artful, and grandmotherly about her mouth as she chattered freely away. And she was not repeating a tale she had told over a dozen times. No journalists had called on her as yet. She spoke straight from the heart, expressing herself by gestures now and then. I took out my notebook because I wanted to have her exact phrases, and half concealed it behind the table as I wrote. But this caution was unnecessary. Madame paid no attention to what I was doing. She raised her finger, and went on:

"Do you know when I saw Anne for the last time? In my own flat. I had made a blue tricot dress for her. When it was ready, she came for it. Naturally we tried it on once more—it looked sweet on her, and I told her so. And what do you think Anne said to that? 'Why of course,' she said; 'after all, it's brand new.'"

Madame van der Waal is a dressmaker by trade, and even at night she does not entirely put aside her dressmaking. I am not referring to her quick, darting hands, nor to the embroidery in her lap; but she moves her head as if she were continually taking measurements of her own words; she studies the style and the fit with blinking eyes; and sometimes her fingers flash to her mouth as though she has a few pins pursed between her lips, so that if necessary she can take a tuck here or there.

ANNE'S SENSE OF HERSELF

She told me that Anne had been a gifted customer—believe it or not, there are such things, she said. There are gifted customers just as there are some very stupid ones. But Anne, she knew very well when something did not fit, and she would say it right out, and no bit of pulling in back or in front would satisfy her. "Aaah!" Madame exclaimed, "she knew who she was. That's it."

I looked startled for a moment, since Madame van der Waal was the first person to say anything like that to me. She sensed at once that this was something arresting.

"Don't you believe it?"

She eyed me sharply.

I quickly asked whether she could remember what color Anne's eyes were. Her father had told me that they were light, I said, but he had been unable to describe them more closely. Madame answered tersely and explicitly: "She had gray-green eyes. Like a cat . . ." she added as the same word shot into my mind, but she instantly gave it a twist as she continued: "Only, cats have veiled eyes, and Anne's were very candid. That is the difference. She could see things—and how! She saw everything exactly as it was, and sometimes she would make a remark—sharp as a needle. Only it did not hurt, because she always hit exactly to the point.

"Margot was entirely different. You would never imagine that two persons could be so very different. Margot was always—*summa cum laude*—all through school, all through life. She, too, was candid and decided, but she was quiet and kind. She was such an exceptional girl that I was always speechless with her. But Anne took after her grandmother, and after her Great-aunt Frank. She was capricious—oh, how capricious!

"You ask whether I had any idea what a writer Anne was? Why, of course. She always wanted to be a writer. No, I wasn't surprised for a moment when I heard about her diary, nor when I saw it. Not the least. Anne was a personality, you understand. And what a personality! Why should such a personality not be able to write, too?"

Madame beamed, and I granted the point, since this is a very broad subject. Whereupon Madame continued:

"She might have gone into the movies, too, of course. Why not? She not only had a gift for being somebody; she also had a gift for representing. My husband was electrified every time she came in at the door—and yet he had two daughters of his own. But the difference was that Anne knew who she was. Our girls didn't. Not even Jopie. . . .

"But Jopie never did know who she was, and yet the two of them were such good friends. They were like a pair of lovers. But Anne had *charme* and self-assurance, while Jopie was *froide, timide.* . . . And still, the plotting and whispering that was always going on between the two of them, and the telephoning all day long, though the Franks lived not three doors away from us. Every morning, there was the telephone ringing—and fifteen minutes later they would be seeing each other in school anyhow. But they never could wait that long."

ANNE—"SHE KNEW WHO SHE WAS"

"When Jopie went to the theater and saw Anne again—the girl must have been wonderful, fascinating, that other girl on the stage—Jopie couldn't say a word when she came home. She went right to bed. . . . She never was really able to express herself, not even as a child, but still and all they were like a pair of lovers with one another. And if Anne spent the weekend with Lies—what jealousy! Indescribable. But if she did not go to see Lies, she came to us, or Jopie went over to the Franks. When Anne came to stay with us, she always brought a suitcase. A suitcase, mind you, when it wasn't a stone's throw between us. The suitcase was empty of course, but Anne insisted on it, because only with the suitcase did she feel as if she were really traveling. And before they went to sleep, the whispering and giggling . . ."

But suddenly Madame drooped a little. She seemed to be looking into herself. After a moment she said:

"You know what has just come to me? I still have the folding bed she used to sleep on. Jopie's was the one we gave away. . . ."

A second passed. I checked my notes. Then I heard Madame's voice:

"So you think Anne did not know who she was?"

Twirling the pencil between my fingers, I replied: "Oh, that is hard to say."

Another moment passed in silence, and I looked toward the window, where night was coming on—as much as night can come in June; it was a darkness full of hidden colors. Then Madame laughed again:

"She knew. Just think, one Sunday, we were just about to sit down to the table, Anne suddenly said good-by. I said: 'Why Anne, we're going to eat now.' But she said no, she had to go home because she had to give Moortje his bath. And I said: 'Why Anne, you're crazy. A cat isn't supposed to be bathed.' But Anne said haughtily: 'Why not? I've often bathed him, and he's never said anything about it!' And she took her suitcase and left.

"Oh no," Madame concluded, "she knew what she wanted. Believe me, she did. And she knew who she was, too."

Thus said Madame van der Waal.

The Voice That Speaks for Six Million

Ilya Ehrenburg

The following excerpt, written by Ilya Ehrenburg, is the foreword to the Russian edition of *Anne Frank: The Diary of a Young Girl*. The outspoken Ehrenburg, who lived much of his life in the former Soviet Union, gained acclaim worldwide as a foreign correspondent, novelist, and literary critic. "One voice out of six million has reached us," says Ehrenburg. That voice belonged to Anne Frank—a child's legacy to an unfeeling and unseeing world. Hers was a voice that proved "stronger than death." The world, however, did not learn. Perpetrators and abettors of the fascist atrocities that killed Anne, her fellow Jews, and others were not held accountable. They escaped punishment and lived to see another day and start another life.

The history of this book is unusual. It appeared in Holland ten years ago, was translated into seventeen languages, and millions of copies have been sold. Plays and films have been made from it; special studies have been written about it.

This is not a novel by a celebrated author, it is the diary of a thirteen-year-old girl; but it affects the reader more profoundly than many masterly works of literature.

Everyone knows that the Hitlerites killed six million Jews, the citizens of twenty countries, rich and poor, famous and unknown. The atom bomb fell on Hiroshima out of the blue, there was no possibility of taking cover. For several years the Hitlerites organized the round-up of millions of people, as wolf battues are organized. The Jews tried to hide; they concealed themselves in quarries, in disused mines, in the holes and corners of towns. They waited days, weeks, months for the final blow to fall. Six million were poisoned in gas chambers, shot in ravines or against fortress walls, condemned to

From Ilya Ehrenburg, "Anne Frank's Diary," in *Chekhov, Stendhal, and Other Essays* (New York: Knopf, 1963). Reprinted courtesy of HarperCollins UK.

slow death by starvation. They were separated from the world by the walls of ghettos, by the barbed wire of concentration camps. Nobody knows what they felt and thought. One voice speaks for six million—the voice not of a sage or a poet but of an ordinary little girl.

A Child's Indictment

Anne Frank kept a diary as girls of her age so often do; on her birthday she was given a thick exercise book and she began to record the events of her young life. Adults decreed that this childish life soon lose its childishness. The diary of one little girl became a human document of tremendous importance and an act of indictment.

What did Anne see? A small attic, where for twenty-five months honest and courageous Dutch people hid eight doomed human beings: the German émigré Otto Frank, his wife, his two daughters Margot and Anne, the Van Daan couple, their son Peter, and the dentist Dussel.

In [Jean-Paul] Sartre's play *No Exit* hell turns out to be an ordinary room in which three sinners are confined forever. Eight people lived in the "secret annexe"; they bickered and quarreled: they were not saints or heroes but quite commonplace people. And Anne recounts their life day by day.

The Toll of Anti-Semitism

Otto Frank was born in Germany; he attended the Lessing Classical Secondary School in Frankfurt am Main and then went into business. During the First World War he was at the front and attained the rank of lieutenant; he took part in one of the bloodiest battles near the French town of Cambrai. He says that he regarded himself as a German; he also says that in his youth, in Frankfurt, where he lived, he had never come across anti-Semitism. He thought his life was established and secure. Then Hitler came to power and everything collapsed like a house of cards. Otto Frank managed to escape to Holland with his family. The girls went to a Dutch school and made friends among the Dutch children. The father realized that he had to start life afresh. He was building a new life when, again, everything collapsed: the German army occupied Holland.

Why was the fury of the fascists turned primarily against the Jews? Vast tomes have been written on this subject, long-winded theories have been put forward, and yet nothing is explained. A mass of age-old prejudices, myths that read like hideous anecdotes, superstitions turned into a philosophical system, envy, ignorance, the necessity to find a scapegoat—all this wove itself into a net that cut Anne off from her little Dutch friends, and six million people from their neighbours and countrymen.

Many books have appeared in various countries telling the story of the heroic rising of the Warsaw ghetto. There were risings, too, in other towns. Among partisan detachments on Soviet territory, in Poland, France, Yugoslavia, Bulgaria, and other countries, the lucky ones who succeeded in escaping from the ghettos fought and died. But millions of Jews were carted away by the Hitlerites to death camps. This was the doom that awaited the Frank family.

There is nothing in Anne's diary that might not have been written by a Dutch, French, or Italian girl. The Hitlerites pinned a six-pointed star on her girlish dress, and she accepted the fact with deep incomprehension but with great dignity.

GROWING UP TO DIE

Some of the pages of the diary make one smile, but the smile quickly fades: the end of the book is all too clearly foreseeable. The thirteen-year-old girl writes that she will give her children a book that she enjoyed; she remarks that life as depicted in novels is very extraordinary—she, for one, would never stay alone with a strange man. This is written by a child who grows up before one's eyes, grows up in the underground, completely walled in. Now she is fifteen, she wants to fall in love; the boy Peter lives in the "annexe" too, and she persuades herself that she is in love with him.

In prison, in concentration camps, people survived terrible ordeals when they had an aim, when they became absorbed in some activity, however illusory. What could an adolescent girl do? Study? Anne tried to study. Play? Anne played—she played at being a writer. She kept a diary, invented stories, started a novel. This uplifted and saved her: of all games she chose the most difficult one, but perhaps the most humanist.

When the reader finishes the diary, he naturally asks: "What became of Anne?" Ernest Schnabel searched through the archives, talked to eye-witnesses, and in his book *The Footsteps of Anne Frank* has related her fate.

Anne's last entry in the diary is dated August 1, 1944: she tries to understand spiritual contradictions.... And in the morning of August 4 Gestapo men broke into the "annexe." The Jews who were hiding there, and the two Dutch people, accused of sheltering them, were taken to prison. A few days later the Jews were transferred to the transit camp of Westerbork. On September 3 a huge transport of Jews was sent from there to Auschwitz. On October 30 Margot and Anne were transferred to the concentration camp of Bergen-Belsen. Margot died of inanition [and typhus] at the end of February 1945. Anne died a few days later.

Their mother died at Auschwitz. Dussel was killed in a gas chamber. Peter was killed. The Van Daan couple died. The Dutchman Koophuis, who was gravely ill, was released shortly after. Kraler was sent to the camp of Amersfoort and, in March 1945, was taken to Germany; he managed to escape.

ONE VOICE OUT OF SIX MILLION

Of the eight Jews who hid in the attic, only Otto Frank survived. When the Soviet army occupied Auschwitz, it saved those few who had not yet been killed. Otto Frank returned to Holland in a roundabout way—via Odessa and Marseilles—but he found none of his people. All he found was Anne's diary.

The Gestapo men looked for valuables; school exercise books did not interest them. The diary had been picked up by two Dutchwomen—Elli and Miep.

To these dry facts I should like to add two stories. Mrs. De Wiek, who was in the transit camp of Westerbork, relates: "I saw Anne and Peter Van Daan every day. They were always together.... Anne's eyes glowed.... And her movements, her looks, had such a lilt to them that I could not help saying to myself: 'She really seems happy.'"

In her diary Anne wrote about a schoolfriend: "Last night, just before I fell asleep, I suddenly saw Lies. She was there, in front of me, clothed in rags, her face thin and worn. Her eyes were very big and she looked at me so sorrowfully and so reproachfully that I could read in her eyes: 'Oh Anne, why have you deserted me? Help, oh help me, rescue me from this hell.'" Anne wrote these lines in November 1943, not knowing what had happened to Lies. But Lies survived. She tells how she met Anne in the Belsen concentration camp: "She was in rags. I saw her thin, emaciated face in the darkness. Her eyes were very big. We cried and cried, for now there was only the barbed wire between us, nothing more."

One voice out of six million has reached us. It is only a child's voice but it has great power, the power of sincerity, of humanity, and also of talent. Not every writer would have been capable of describing both the inhabitants of the "annexe" and his own feelings as Anne succeeded in doing.

On March 29, 1944, Anne wrote: "Bolkestein, a Minister, was speaking on the Dutch programme from London and he said that after the war they ought to make a collection of letters and diaries. Of course, they all immediately pounced on my diary. Just imagine how interesting it would be if I were to publish a romance of the 'Secret Annexe.' The title alone would be enough to make people take it for a detective novel. But, seriously, how funny it would seem after the war, in ten years' time, if we Jews were to tell how we lived and what we ate and talked about here. . . ."

A Lesson Not Learned, Crimes Not Punished

Since then, not ten but sixteen years have passed. Anne was mistaken: recently swastikas have been reappearing on the walls of European towns. In Western Germany there are people who say quite openly: "A pity that Hitler didn't finish them off"—they are sorry that Anne's father was not killed too.

In Hitler's days the "Racial Purity" Laws were formulated by Dr. Hans Globke. There are six million innocent victims on his conscience. Six million have perished, and Dr. Hans Globke is [German] Chancellor Adenauer's right-hand man; he is responsible for allocating funds for propaganda purposes.

When the Hitlerites invaded Holland, another doctor, Hermann Konring, was appointed Reich Commissioner for the Occupied Netherlands. Every movement of his was watched with horror by Anne Frank and her parents. How has Dr. Hermann Konring been punished for the blood and tears of Anne Frank? Today he is a deputy of the Bundestag, a member of the Christian Democratic Party now in power. I repeat: he is not in some attic, not in some den, but in the Parliament of the Federal German Republic.

Anne was in the Westerbork transit camp. There, parties of the doomed were formed. Westerbork camp was under SS Albert Konrad Hemecker, who lives at present in Düsseldorf.

It was in this town that members of the Peace Movement were brought to trial. In this town they do not try the commandants of concentration camps; and in his old age Albert Konrad Hemecker has taken to commerce. . . .

The moral is clear: one can with impunity, right in the twentieth century, do to death old people and children, murder them with poison gas, then maintain a tactful silence and lie low, and fifteen years later watch with satisfaction the goose-stepping of young would-be executioners and murderers.

Anne Frank confessed that she was not particularly interested in politics. She did not play at tribunals and parliaments. She wanted to live. She dreamed of love; she would have been a good mother. They killed her.

Millions of readers know Anne Frank as if she had been to their homes. Six million perfectly innocent people perished. One clear, child's voice lives on: it has proved stronger than death.

Anne Frank's *Diary:*
A Story That Endures

Lawrence Elliott

In the United States *Anne Frank: The Diary of a
Young Girl* has never been out of print since it was
first published almost five decades ago. The Secret
Annex in Amsterdam, where the diary was written,
is now the Anne Frank House and visitors flock to
see the memorabilia exhibited there. The following
excerpt written by Lawrence Elliot, an author of
several books, an editor of *Coronet* magazine, and
a staff writer for *Reader's Digest*, makes clear the
circumstances and events that formed the world of
the teenage Anne Frank. The prose of the diary
remains today a haunting reminder of a young girl's
indomitable spirit and the frightening reality of her
loss. Elliott maintains that Anne Frank remains to
this day "a candle in the dark to the rest of us."

Early on a wintry, wet morning in Amsterdam, a cluster of
people huddle under umbrellas outside the unremarkable
four story building at No. 263 Prinsengracht. Rain or shine,
there are always visitors here during the day, sometimes a
double line reaching to the corner. They wait their turn to
climb the steep stairway to the secret annex where just over
50 years ago a young girl named Anne Frank wrote the diary
that caught the hearts of people everywhere.

The annex at the rear of the building has four small rooms
on two floors, with an attic above. The desperate souls who
went into hiding here from the Nazis are long gone. But half
a century after they were betrayed and captured by the
Nazis, their story, thanks to Anne's writing, still endures.

They were eight, two families and one other adult, confined in this space for 25 months, people who went to sleep
and woke up afraid, who got on one another's nerves and

From Lawrence Elliot, "Anne Frank's Enduring Gift." Reprinted with permission from
the May 1995 *Reader's Digest.* Copyright ©1995 by The Reader's Digest Assn., Inc.

whose endless hours of boredom were repeatedly shattered by bolts of stupefying terror.

But Anne's spirit was never broken. Just three weeks before the end, she told with stunning perception why her convictions remained intact:

> I still believe, in spite of everything, that people are truly good at heart. It's utterly impossible for me to build my life on a foundation of chaos, suffering and death. I see the world being slowly transformed into a wilderness. I hear the approaching thunder. I feel the suffering of millions. And yet, when I look up at the sky, I somehow feel that this cruelty will end and that peace and tranquillity will return.

When the diary was published, its ringing *yes* to life in the fact of death stirred the compassion of far-flung millions. Since its original Dutch publication, the diary has been translated into 55 languages and has sold 25 million copies. In the United States *The Diary of a Young Girl* has never been out of print.

Nothing underscores Anne's lasting relevance more than the numbers of people—9000 in 1960, 600,000 [in 1994]—who come to visit this quiet house.

THE MOVE TO AMSTERDAM

Anneliese Marie Frank was born on June 12, 1929, in Frankfurt-am-Main, Germany, where her Jewish family had lived for generations. Her father, Otto Heinrich Frank, had been an officer in the German army during World War I, but when Hitler came to power, scapegoating the Jews for Germany's woes, he decided to move his family to Amsterdam. There, by December 1940, he'd set up a spices and herbs business in the creaky 17th-century building at 263 Prinsengracht on a tree-lined canal. His small staff valued him as a fair and considerate employer.

The first years in Amsterdam were happy for Anne. In the pleasant suburb where the Franks lived, the German past receded, and she grew more and more Dutch. It was commonly held that her sister Margot, three years older, was brighter and prettier, but Anne, with her quick wit and charm, was more popular and outspoken. She liked movies, Greek mythology and boys.

In May 1940 Hitler's armies swept into the neutral Netherlands. Police roundups of Jews began nine months later, and in September 1941 Anne and Margot had to transfer to an all-Jewish school. The following April Jews were compelled to sew a yellow star onto their clothing.

THE START OF THE DIARY

On June 12, 1942, Anne started writing in her diary. A slender volume with a red and white plaid cover, it had been given to her by her parents for her 13th birthday. The earliest entries were filled with bubbly classroom gossip, but within a week she was writing:

> June 20. Jews were required to turn in their bicycles. Jews were forbidden to use streetcars and to ride in cars, even their own. Jews were forbidden to be out on the streets between 8 p.m. and 6 a.m.—forbidden even to sit in their gardens after 8 p.m.

Anne's father had been making preparations to take his family into hiding in the unused rooms beneath the attic of 263 Prinsengracht. On Sundays Otto had spirited household necessities, furniture and boxes of canned food up to the secret annex. Knowing outside help would be essential, he confided in four employees—Johannes Kleiman, Victor Kugler and two young secretaries, Miep Gies and Bep Voskuijl. Anne wrote:

> July 5. A few days ago Father began to talk about going into hiding. He sounded so serious that I felt scared. "Don't you worry," he said. "Just enjoy your carefree life while you can." Oh, may these somber words not come true for as long as possible!

THE SECRET ANNEX

Only hours after Anne made this diary entry, an SS call-up order was delivered to 16-year-old Margot Frank. She was to report the following afternoon for transport to a labor camp in Germany. Delay was no longer possible. Early the next morning the entire Frank family simply disappeared. Margot went first. She stripped off her yellow star and pedaled a contraband bicycle into a hard summer rain alongside Miep Gies to the hiding place. Anne and her parents followed on foot,

> each of us with a school bag and a shopping bag filled to the brim with the most varied assortment of items.

They had walked away from everything they cared about in the world except each other. Days later, by pre-arrangement, they were joined in the hideout by another imperiled Jewish family, Hermann van Pels, a business colleague of Otto's, his wife and their 15-year-old son, Peter. By this time, a rumor was circulating that the Franks had escaped to Switzerland.

> July 11. It is like being on vacation in some strange board-inghouse. It may be damp and lopsided, but there's probably not a more comfortable hiding place in all of the Netherlands. Up to now our bedroom, with its blank walls, was very bare. But thanks to Father, who brought my movie-star collection, I was able to plaster the walls with pictures.

This long, narrow room shared by Anne and Margot was next to their parents' bedroom; the Van Pels family occupied the other two rooms. A specially made revolving bookcase concealed the only entrance to the secret annex, and there were blackout curtains on every window.

Inside, the most extreme cautions were in force with regard to cooking, garbage disposal and use of the single toilet. Everyone whispered during the workday for fear of being overheard by the firms' warehousemen, who knew nothing of the fugitives living over their heads. They moved about—in stockinged feet—only when it was absolutely necessary.

The summer of 1942 passed in a procession of tedious days. In November Miep came to tell them that their dentist, Fritz Pfeffer, was desperate for a place to hide. Margot moved in with her parents, and soon Anne was sharing her room with the newcomer.

The four faithful employees visited after the other workers had left the building and brought food and hard-to-get necessities—soap, toothpaste, aspirin. They also supplied books and magazines. "Never have they uttered a single word about the burden we must be," Anne wrote.

Anne begged for news of her friends and their families, but it was never good. Over the clandestine radio came BBC reports of mass deportations. When Pfeffer arrived, he told them how the Germans were ringing at every door looking for Jews.

> When it's dark, I often see long lines of good, innocent people walking on and on. All are marched to their death. I feel wicked sleeping in a warm bed and get frightened when I think of close friends now at the mercy of the cruelest monsters ever to stalk the earth. And all because they are Jews!

Later she wrote, "But I'll say no more on the subject. My own thoughts give me nightmares!"

Her nightmares were real enough. Once when burglars broke into the warehouse, police came and searched the building while the eight huddled together in the secret annex.

Footsteps on the staircase, then a rattling at the bookcase! "Now we're done for!" I said. Then the footsteps receded. We were out of danger—so far.

When Anne had filled every page of the diary, Miep brought her loose sheets and blank accounting books from the office, and the writing went on. The diary was her best friend, she wrote, and she let her imagination run free, as she herself could not. "I feel like a songbird whose wings have been ripped off and who keeps hurling itself against the bars of its dark cage." Two months after writing that, she wondered, "Will anyone ever understand that I am simply a teen-ager badly in need of some good plain fun?"

At first Anne had dismissed 15-year-old Peter van Pels as "a shy, awkward boy whose company won't amount to much." But by the spring of 1944, when she was nearly 15, they had fallen in love. They often met in the attic, where a window looked out onto the blue sky. From this window they could see the top of a greening chestnut tree and sea gulls gliding on the wind.

> April 16. Remember yesterday's date. Isn't it an important day for every girl when she gets her first kiss? . . . Father wants me to stop going upstairs so often, but I like being with Peter. I trust him.

She was reading widely—"Oh, there's still so much to find out and learn"—and she aspired to write a book to be called *The Secret Annex* based on her diary.

> To become a journalist—that's what I want! I know I can write. I want to go on living even after my death! And that's why I am so grateful to God for having given me this gift, which I can use to express all that's inside me!

At 8 a.m. on June 6, 1944, the BBC broadcast news of the Allied landings in Normandy. Hope surged through the annex. Could this be the year of victory and liberation? Could it be, Anne fantasized, that she would be back in school for the new term? A few days later she celebrated her 15th birthday.

BETRAYAL AT THE ANNEX

The end came on Friday morning, August 4, after they had passed 761 days in hiding. Around 10:30 a car drew up at 263 Prinsengracht, and plainclothes police led by a uniformed policeman ran in. With guns drawn, they forced Victor Kugler to lead them to the fake bookcase and commanded him to open it. Moments later the eight Jews were under arrest. A covered truck came and took them, Kugler and Johannes Kleiman away.

The two secretaries, Miep Gies and Bep Voskuijl, waited until late in the afternoon before going to the secret annex. The Nazis had ransacked the place. Miep began picking up papers from the floor. Soon she was holding something of incomparably greater worth than the money and jewelry taken—Anne's diary.

A DAUGHTER'S LEGACY

A month later the eight Prinsengracht fugitives were put on the last train to carry prisoners from the Netherlands to Auschwitz. There the men and women were separated, never to see one another again.

Anne and Margot were transported to Bergen-Belsen in central Germany, where, like tens of thousands of others, they fell victim to typhus. Anne tended Margot until the very end and died after her sister in March 1945—a few weeks before British troops entered the camp.

Who had betrayed them back in Amsterdam? Possibly a new warehouseman, curious about the upper floors, who would have coveted the bounty paid by the Nazis for every Jew turned in. Though the man was investigated twice, charges were never brought against him.

Kleiman and Kugler were imprisoned in the Netherlands, but eventually returned to work at 263 Prinsengracht.

Otto Frank, the only one of the eight Jews to survive, was freed from Auschwitz by the Soviet army in January 1945. Eventually he made his way back to Amsterdam, where he went to live with Miep Gies and her husband, Jan. When they heard of Anne's death, Miep gave him the diary. "Here is your daughter's legacy to you," she said.

It took Otto Frank a long time to finish reading it. Then slowly, painfully, he began typing out a copy for friends and relatives to read. A year later it was published under Anne's title, *The Secret Annex*, and her wish to become a writer was fulfilled.

Anne's strong, honest prose—scrupulously revised by her, fired with the tension of a fine novel—will always be an aching reminder of what we lost when she was cut down. As someone wrote in one of the visitors' books at 263 Prinsengracht, "If I could have only two books for the rest of my life, they would be the Bible and *The Diary of Anne Frank.*"

Soon people began knocking at the door of No. 263, asking to see the secret annex. But within a few years the place was earmarked for redevelopment. Only a public uproar saved it from demolition. A foundation was established to raise money for the restoration of the building, which would include an exhibition area. On May 3, 1960, the Anne Frank House was officially opened to visitors.

Today, squeezing past the revolving bookcase, one enters the Franks' bedroom. Still hanging on the wall is the map of Normandy on which Otto traced the advance of the Allied armies. Next to the map are the penciled lines by which he charted the growth of the three children who would never attain adulthood.

Anne's room is next. Her movie-star pictures are still pasted to the wall, faded photos that let cheer and illusion into her prison. It is hard not to feel Anne's presence here. Many leave the room in tears.

An American college student who traveled from London especially to see the Anne Frank House said, "She faced death in this place and still joked in her diary and dreamed of a life after the war. It shows that it isn't how or when you die that matters—it's how you live your life."

Otto Frank died in 1980 at the age of 91. Of all those who witnessed the drama of the secret annex, only Miep Gies is still living. Now 85, she has said that every day of her life she wishes things had been different, "that even if Anne's diary had been lost to the world, Anne and the others might somehow have been saved."

"I still believe, in spite of everything, that people are truly good at heart," wrote Anne. She remains to this day a candle in the dark for us all.

The *Diary* Inspires Antidiscrimination Efforts

Ian Barnes

In 1985, more than forty years after the death of Anne Frank in a Nazi concentration camp, writer Ian Barnes published an article in *History Today* magazine on the impact of Anne Frank and her *Diary*. In the following excerpt, Barnes focuses on the how and why of the creation of the non-Jewish Anne Frank Foundation in Amsterdam, the preservation of the Anne Frank House and what purpose each serves. Anne Frank has survived as a symbol and martyr of Nazi atrocity and a writer of literary worth. Neo-Nazi groups and racism continue to exist in Europe and elsewhere as do other forms of discrimination. The insight into injustice portrayed in the *Diary* serves to combat such discrimination and contributes to the obliteration of contemporary injustice.

On 4th April, 1944, Anne Frank wrote, 'I want to go on living even after my death!' Four months later, she and her family left for a concentration camp after capture by the Gestapo, and she died from typhus at Bergen-Belsen in March 1945, aged fifteen years.

Anne Frank is chiefly known for her Diary, with approximately eighteen million copies sold, in fifty-two editions, in over fifty languages (including Japanese, Ladino, and Serbo-Croat). A play and a film based on the Diary ensured that its ideals and poignant drama reached a wider audience. However, Anne Frank has lived on as an impetus behind the Anne Frank Foundation in Amsterdam, propagating the aspirations bequeathed to the world by the Diary through its educational work; as a symbol and martyr of Nazi atrocity; as a target for extreme right-wing attempts to

From Ian Barnes, "Forty Years On," *History Today*, March 1985, pp. 48–50. Reprinted by permission of *History Today*.

whitewash the past; and as a writer with literary and documentary value.

EFFECTS OF ANTI-SEMITISM

In 1933, the Frank family fled from Germany and its anti-Semitic atmosphere to Amsterdam where Otto Frank, Anne's father, set up a firm. . . . The German invasion of Holland in Spring 1940 threatened all who had sought sanctuary in Holland. In March 1941, German occupation forces issued a decree making it possible for Jewish businesses to be controlled and sold. . . . Further anti-Jewish laws followed constructing an anti-Semitic apartheid system in public places, the banning of secondary education for Jews, and ultimately the deportation of Jews to Auschwitz and other camps. For the Jews, survival depended on hiding.

Otto Frank succeeded in this thanks to the aid of his former staff. . . . [They] prepared a refuge . . . known as the Annex. A moveable bookcase concealed its entrance, serving as a back wall of a hall used as storage space. When the German order arrived on July 5th, 1942, for Anne's sister, Margot, to report for a work-camp, the family immediately moved into the Annex with another family of three people, later joined by one more person. The former staff, all Gentiles, became responsible for supplying the families. During office hours, the Annex inmates had to make no sound. Anne, who was thirteen on June 12th, described the following twenty-five months in her Diary.

ANNE FRANK'S DIARY AND ITS IMPACT

Anne had begun this journal shortly before entering the Annex. It documents the privations experienced, including periods when the daily diet comprised two spoonfuls of porridge plus rotten potatoes, spinach and lettuce. The Diary evokes the terror, personal relationships, a young girl's perception, tempered by an adult compassion, humanity and love of justice, together with an implicit forgiveness for the Nazi authors of their predicament and occupation of Holland. Various references were made to the anger and horror of war, to anti-Semitism, contrasted with the growing self-awareness of an adolescent girl possessing a quiet courage of an individual human being faced by a hostile world.

On August 4th, 1944, a German policeman with four Dutch accomplices entered Prinsengracht 263 to arrest

those in hiding. Betrayal was involved. The Annex inmates
. . . were transported to the police station. The traitor was
never discovered. After the arrest, Miep and Elly [two of the
helpers] . . . found the Diary and gave it to Otto Frank in the
summer of 1945, he being the sole survivor from the Annex.
In 1947, Otto Frank published parts of the Diary, then entitled *Het Achterhuis* (The Secret Annex).

The impact of the Diary has been immense, especially on
younger generations, school children, adolescents, and students. In Germany, a type of Anne Frank cult developed in
the fifties similar to movements started by St Teresa and St
Bernadette. In 1957, mass emotion was channelled into a
pilgrimage of two thousand young people, mainly from
Hamburg, to Bergen-Belsen where, in pouring rain during
the course of a ceremony, flowers were placed on the mass
graves—in one of which Anne Frank was buried.

One should not be surprised that the twelve years of Nazi
degradation suffered by Europe, highlighted in the diary of
a Jewish girl, has generated attacks on the Diary's veracity
by neo-Nazi groups in various countries. These remnants of
the past, and their more youthful heirs, seek to rehabilitate
Nazism by denying the responsibility of their ideology for
mass murder. To prove the Diary a fraud, a hoax, would call
into question the extermination of millions of people, and
Nazi war guilt. In some neo-Nazi eyes, the camps and ovens
were fabricated by the Allies to be used as evidence at the
Nuremberg War Crimes Tribunals against the true defend-
ers of Western civilisation—as some Nazis saw themselves
in their Russian campaign. . . .

THE ANNE FRANK FOUNDATION

The Anne Frank Foundation was created and uses civic education to counter the spread of this resurgent anti-Semitic
and politically suspect material, and to prevent Europe facing any re-enactment of the atrocities of the Second World
War. On May 3rd, 1957, the Foundation was established with
the purpose of . . . preserving the Annex from redevelopment
and keeping it as a shrine for the many pilgrims visiting it.
The house receives nearly four hundred thousand visitors
annually. The Foundation's goal is the promotion of Anne
Frank's ideals interpreted as combatting prejudice, discrimination and repression and striving to establish democracy
in all countries. . . .

The Annex is preserved as a three-dimensional document portraying the tragedy of the Frank family and symbolising the grief and fear of the persecuted. This has formed the setting for exhibitions on anti-Semitism, Nazism, and the post-1945 extreme right. Two such were *The Ultra-Right in Western Europe* and *Neo-Nazis and the Denial of the Holocaust.* On June 12th, 1985, the Foundation is mounting an exhibition in the Public Library in New York and in the Historical Museum in Frankfurt, Germany. Its contents reflect the life of Anne Frank, the process of Nazi *Gleichschaltung* in Germany after 1933, the persecution of Jews, life in occupied Holland, the liberation, and the hope for a better world, and racism and anti-Semitism now. One photograph admirably illustrates the permeation of Nazi images in everyday life: a small child gazes at a Christmas tree hung with pretty glass baubles—Nazi swastikas. The past is a warning for the present and the considerable violation of human rights in the world.

A documentation centre compiles information on these matters and relies on individual good-will—journalists, politicians and Euro-MPs—in investigating the activities of neo-Fascist groups. Thus, this non-Jewish Foundation hopes to clarify for young people what Fascism and Nazism was and is, especially in times of economic recession when the young are noticeably hard hit and provide an alluring target for Neo-Nazi propaganda. . . .

A major instrument for the Foundation's social education is the Anne Frank newspaper. Three versions exist of this carefully constructed twelve page journal. They explain the development of Nazi Germany and the origins of the Second World War and use the occupation of Holland as a springboard for articles on Nazi racism and the danger of still active neo-Nazi groups in contemporary Europe. . . .

The story of Anne Frank is the focal point of the papers, teenagers readily identifying with the authoress. The newspapers avoid the use of sensational examples of horror, and the history of wartime persecution is well written. For example, extracts from a letter sent by a chemical company to Auschwitz concentration camp requesting one hundred and fifty women as guinea pigs for testing a new sleeping pill are skilfully deployed. Two hundred marks were offered for each healthy woman and one hundred and seventy marks for those in poor health. This chilling business letter is followed by a laconic statement that all the women have died and can the company have a new 'batch'. . . .

ANNE'S INSPIRATION FOR THE FUTURE

On April 11th, 1944, Anne Frank wrote, 'If God lets me live, I shall achieve more than mother ever did, I shall not remain insignificant, I shall work in the world for people.' This month is the fortieth anniversary of Anne's death and her hopes remain alive. The best-selling Diary has gripped the world displaying the truth and purity of the expectations and desire of a young Jewish girl. The Foundation's Chairman . . . said that her hope for the future banishes despair, her insight into the injustice of her time contributes to the eradication of injustice now.

The Foundation's work is inspired by Anne Frank's testimony. On July 15th, 1944, three weeks before her arrest, she wrote:

> It's really a wonder that I haven't dropped all my ideals because they seem so absurd and impossible to implement. Yet I keep them, because in spite of everything I still believe that people are really good at heart. I simply can't build up my hopes on a foundation consisting of confusion, misery and death. I see the world gradually being turned into a wilderness, I hear the ever-approaching thunder which will destroy us too, I can feel the suffering of millions and yet, if I look up into the heavens, I think that it will all come right, that this cruelty too will end, and that peace and tranquillity will return again. In the meantime, I must uphold my ideals for perhaps the time will come when I shall be able to carry them out.

CHRONOLOGY

1925

Otto Frank and Edith Holländer marry.

1926

Margot Frank is born in Frankfurt-am-Main, Germany.

1929

Anneliese Marie (Anne) Frank is born June 12 in Frankfurt-am-Main, Germany.

1933

Adolf Hitler becomes chancellor of Germany, putting the Nazis (National Socialist German Workers Party) in power; the Holocaust begins.

1934

The Franks flee to Amsterdam to escape Nazi persecution; Anne begins Montessori schooling; Hitler proclaims himself führer of the Third Reich, a Nazi dictatorship in Germany.

1937

The Van Pels family (called in the *Diary* Van Daan) flees to the Netherlands.

1938

Hitler annexes Austria; Fritz Pfeffer (called in the *Diary* Alfred Dussel) flees to the Netherlands.

1939

Hitler's armies invade Poland, setting off World War II; the Dutch government proclaims its neutrality.

1940

German troops occupy the Netherlands and invade Denmark, Norway, Belgium, and Luxembourg; France surrenders to Germany; Otto Frank's company moves to a building on Amsterdam's Prinsengracht Canal.

1941

Nazi laws are extended to Holland, forcing Anne and Margot to attend the Jewish Lyceum instead of the Montessori school; the people of Amsterdam protest abuse directed against the Jews; Germany invades Rumania, Bulgaria, Greece, and the Soviet Union; the Japanese attack Pearl Harbor.

1942

Anne's parents give her a diary for her thirteenth birthday in which she starts writing letters to "Dear Kitty"; Margot Frank is ordered to report for deportation; the Franks go into hiding in a "secret annex" in the building where Otto Frank works; the Van Pels family and Fritz Pfeffer move in with the Franks.

1943

The Germans retreat from the Soviet Union.

1944

Anne begins editing her diary; the Allies invade Germany; the Gestapo raid the Secret Annex and arrest the eight Jews hidden there; the Franks are sent to Westerbork, a transit camp for Jews, and then to Auschwitz, a Nazi concentration camp in Poland; Anne and Margot are sent to Bergen-Belsen, a camp in Germany; Hermann Van Pels dies in Auschwitz and Fritz Pfeffer in Neuengamme.

1945

Anne and Margot contract typhus and die in Bergen-Belsen; Edith Frank and Peter Van Pels and his mother die in camps; Hitler commits suicide, and Germany surrenders; World War II ends; Otto Frank is liberated, returns to Amsterdam, and is given Anne's diary.

1947

Anne's diary is published in Dutch in Amsterdam under the title *Het Achterhuis* (*The Secret Annex*).

1952

Anne's diary is published in the United States as *Anne Frank: The Diary of a Young Girl.*

1955

A play based on Anne's diary opens in New York and wins the Pulitzer Prize for drama.

1956

The German version of the play opens to packed audiences.

1960

Anne's hiding place, converted to a museum called the Anne Frank House, is opened to the public.

1980

Otto Frank dies.

1986

The Critical Edition of the *Diary* is published by the Dutch Department of War Documentation.

1989

The Diary of Anne Frank: The Critical Edition is published in the United States and Anne's diaries are confirmed authentic.

1995

The fiftieth anniversary of Anne Frank's death; *The Definitive Edition* of the *Diary* is published in the United States.

FOR FURTHER RESEARCH

EDITIONS OF *THE DIARY OF A YOUNG GIRL* AND OTHER WORKS BY ANNE FRANK

David Barnouw and Gerrold van der Stroom, eds., Arnold J. Pomerans and B.M. Mooyaart-Doubleday, trans., prepared by the Netherlands State Institute for War Documentation, *The Diary of Anne Frank: The Critical Edition.* New York: Doubleday, 1989.

Anne Frank, *The Works of Anne Frank.* Westport, CT: Greenwood Press, 1977.

Otto H. Frank and Mirjam Pressler, eds., Susan Massotty, trans., *The Diary of a Young Girl: The Definitive Edition.* New York: Doubleday, 1995.

Ralph Manheim and Michael Mok, *Anne Frank's Tales from the Secret Annex.* Garden City, NY: Doubleday, 1959.

B.M. Mooyaart-Doubleday, trans., introduction by Eleanor Roosevelt, *Anne Frank: The Diary of a Young Girl.* Garden City, NY: Doubleday, 1952.

ABOUT ANNE FRANK AND *THE DIARY OF A YOUNG GIRL*

Books

David A. Adler, *A Picture Book of Anne Frank.* New York: Holiday House, 1993.

Anne Frank Educational Trust, *Dear Anne Frank.* London: Puffin Books, 1995.

John Berryman, *The Freedom of the Poet.* New York: Farrar, Straus, and Giroux, 1976.

Gene Brown, *Anne Frank, Child of the Holocaust.* Woodbridge, CT: Blackbirch Press, 1991.

Steven A. Cohen, *Anne Frank in the World.* Amsterdam: Anne Frank Foundation, 1985.

Dennis B. Fradin, *Remarkable Children: Twenty Who Made History.* Boston: Little, Brown, 1987.

Miep Gies, with Alison Leslie Gold, *Anne Frank Remembered: The Story of the Woman Who Helped to Hide the Frank Family.* New York: Simon and Schuster, 1987.

Frances Goodrich, *The Diary of Anne Frank,* dramatized by Frances Goodrich and Albert Hackett. New York: Random House, 1956.

Lawrence Graver, *An Obsession with Anne Frank: Meyer Levin and the Diary.* Berkeley: University of California Press, 1995.

Sandor Katz, *Anne Frank.* New York: Chelsea House, 1996.

De I. Jong, *The Origin of the Diary.* Amsterdam: Frank Fehmers Production, 1970.

Meyer Levin, *The Obsession.* New York: Simon and Schuster, 1973.

Willy Lindwer, *The Last Seven Months of Anne Frank.* New York: Anchor Books, 1992.

Eva Schloss, *Eva's Story.* New York: St. Martin's Press, 1988.

Ernst Schnabel, *Anne Frank: A Portrait in Courage,* Richard and Clara Winston, trans. New York: Harcourt, Brace, 1958.

Anna G. Steenmeijer, ed., with Otto Frank and Henri van Praag, *A Tribute to Anne Frank.* New York: Doubleday, 1970.

Rund van der Rol and Rian Verhoeven, in association with the Anne Frank House, Tony Langham and Plym Peters, trans., introduction by Anna Quindlen, *Anne Frank, Beyond the Diary: A Photographic Remembrance.* New York: Viking, 1993.

Cara Wilson, *Love, Otto: The Legacy of Anne Frank.* Kansas City, MO: Andrews and McMeel, 1995.

Journals and Periodicals

Hyman A. Enzer, "The Diary of Anne Frank: The Critical Edition," *Contemporary Sociology,* March 1991.

Sander L. Gilman, "The Dead Child Speaks: Reading the Diary of Anne Frank," *Studies in American Jewish Literature,* vol. 7, no. 1, Spring 1988.

Sylvania Patterson Iskander, "Anne Frank's Reading," *Children's Literature Association Quarterly*, vol. 13, no. 3, Fall 1988.

Hieke Jippes, "Anne Frank Revisited," *World Press Review*, June 1981.

Gaynor Jones, "Anne Frank's Diary: The Epilogue," *Maclean's*, September 29, 1980.

About the Holocaust

Susan B. Bachrach, *Tell Them We Remember: The Story of the Holocaust*. Boston: Little, Brown, 1994.

Michael Berenbaum, *The World Must Know: The History of the Holocaust as Told in the United States Holocaust Memorial Museum*. Boston: Little, Brown, 1993.

Miriam Chaikin, *A Nightmare in History: The Holocaust 1933–1945*. New York: Clarion Books, 1987.

Abraham Resnick, *The Holocaust*. San Diego: Lucent Books, 1991.

Karen Shawn, *The End of Innocence: Anne Frank and the Holocaust*. New York: Braun Center for Holocaust Studies, Anti-Defamation League of B'nai B'rith, 1994.

United States Holocaust Memorial Council, *Fifty Years Ago: Revolt Amid the Darkness*. Washington, DC: United States Holocaust Memorial Museum, 1993.

INDEX